The 60-Second Philosopher

About the Author

Andrew Pessin is Chair of Philosophy at Connecticut College. He is author of *The God Question: What famous thinkers from Plato to Dawkins have said about the divine*. He has appeared several times on *The David Letterman Show* as "The Genius".

The 60-Second Philosopher

Expand your mind on a minute or so a day!

Andrew Pessin

ONEWORLD
OXFORD

A Oneworld Paperback Original

Published by Oneworld Publications 2009

Copyright © Andrew Pessin 2009

The right of Andrew Pessin to be identified as the
Author of this work has been asserted by him in
accordance with the Copyright, Designs and Patents Act 1988

ISBN 978–1–85168–688–9

Typeset by Jayvee, Trivandrum, India
Cover design by Patrick Knowles
Printed and bound in Great Britain
by Bell & Bain, Glasgow

Oneworld Publications
185 Banbury Road
Oxford OX2 7AR
England
www.oneworld-publications.com

Learn more about Oneworld. Join our mailing list to
find out about our latest titles and special offers at:
www.oneworld-publications.com

Some philosophers believe there is a reason for everything.
This book is dedicated to my three reasons for everything:
ERP, NRP, and GR

CONTENTS

INTRODUCTION

This book is for the philosopher in you.

You may not be aware that there is one, you may not think you *want* there to be one, but I can assure you not only that there is—but also that, once you let him (or her) out for a bit, you'll be more than glad you did. For philosophy can take you to some pretty amazing places, all without leaving your arm-chair or spot on the 7:13 a.m. train; and it can show you some pretty amazing things, even without your looking very far. In fact it can show you that the places you go and the things you see each and every day are already pretty amazing. It can thus sharpen your appreciation of the world—and your mind—at the same time.

And best of all, it can do this on just a minute (or so) a day.

True, some really smart thinkers have been debating philo-sophical questions for nearly three millennia now, with the work continuing at a fevered pitch even as we speak. But few people these days have the time to plow through three thousand years worth of philosophical writings—not to mention master the Greek and Latin and Hebrew and French and German and maybe even Urdu necessary to grapple with the originals.

This book was designed so that you don't have to.

In its concise chapters I hope it will get you to some of those amazing places and show you some of those amazing things— by getting you to think outside the box, and inside the box, and about the whole idea of boxes.

Of course the first decision to make, in composing the book, was exactly what to include. Well, when you ask two philosophers (they say) you get at least three opinions. So, seeking advice on this book, I asked some seventeen philosophers and received, accordingly, about twenty-five-and-a-half different opinions.* Fortunately they all conflicted with each other about a dozen different ways so I could pretty much ignore everything they said. Instead I asked the philosopher within myself what *he* thought, and the result was the sixty or so opinions constituting this book. Of course they too all conflict with

* My great thanks go to Gabriella Rothman, Andrew Postman, Ed McManus, Mairav Rothstein, Barbara Clas, Emma Matthieson, Kerey McKenna, Adam Weber, Jeff Nemec, Sarah Wilson, Joaquin Espinoza, Will Henrich, Ian Barnes, Casey Johnson, Shelly Alminas, Meekah Rothman, and especially my editor at Oneworld, Mike Harpley.

each other a dozen different ways, so I asked him if that's something I should worry about it. I suppose I shouldn't have been surprised when he answered, "Well, it is and it isn't."

That's how things are, in the world of philosophy.

For the conflict of opinions *is* something to worry about when you have to make up your mind about some important problem, since at that time all conflict must be resolved. But until that time you will generally find that an awfully good case can be made for one answer and an awfully good case can be made for an opposing answer. A particular idea might seem appealing until you suddenly come up with an objection to it; but then you might almost as quickly think of a way to respond to the objection. Philosophical reflection is like that: not static, and fixed, but ongoing and dynamic. The conflict of opinions not only *isn't* something to worry about, in fact, it is precisely how things ought to be. For only after you've considered a particular issue from all sides will you be able meaningfully to decide what you think.

This book will give you a lot of sides, of a lot of things, to think about.

You will find herein a healthy sample of some of the major questions, problems, issues, and ideas that have been keeping philosophers busy, in some cases, for nearly three millennia. The essays cover a wide range of topics, from mind to body, from space and time to causation and free will, from knowledge and reason to skepticism and the senses, from absolute morality to relative morality to the complete rejection of morality, from God to godlessness, and more. Though they are related to each other in various ways and sometimes reference each other, they are also quite self-sufficient and may be read individually, in any order. Most importantly the thoughts within are presented as they present themselves to the philosopher who is grappling with them: in a personal way, in a *first*-personal way, as a puzzle or a paradox or a problem that demands resolution as compellingly as it seems to resist it. So it's no surprise, indeed, that you will often discover arguments leaning in opposite ways, leading towards opposing sides of the issue in question, since that is just how thinking itself naturally proceeds.

For again, only after you've considered all sides will you be in a meaningful position to choose one—when that time comes to decide.

And unfortunately, alas, the philosopher within me cannot make that decision for you. His job, he reminds me, is merely to rouse the philosopher within *you* and to get you thinking—not to tell you what to think.

That's *your* philosopher's job.

1

THE PHILOSOPHER WITHIN YOU

There's the legend of the fish who swam around asking every sea creature he'd meet, "Where is this great ocean I keep hearing about?" A pretty small legend, true—but one with a pretty big message.

We are very much like that fish.

For consider, it's hard to look at a newborn baby without thinking: what an incredible miracle. But when was the last time you looked at an adult and had the same thought? But why not? Every adult *was* a little baby; if the latter is a miracle then so is the former. But it never occurs to us to think this way for one simple reason: we're so used to seeing people that we stop reflecting on them.

Or you drop something, a spoon, and it falls to the floor. But why? Couldn't it, in theory, have remained floating in air or moved upwards? And *how* exactly does it fall to the floor, by "gravity"? There are no strings connecting the earth to the spoon. How can the earth pull on something from a distance, that it's not even attached to? Why don't we pause every time something drops and say: what an incredible miracle!

The most ordinary things contain a whole lifetime of questions, if only we are reminded to start asking them.

Children already know to ask these questions. Every answer you provide to one of their "Why?" questions just generates the next question. But we were all children once. What we need to do now is to let the child still within us—the philosopher within us—re-emerge. What we need now are a few seconds out of our ordinary conceptual habits. We need to take a cold wet plunge into the great deep ocean of thought.

It's time to start thinking.

RELATED CHAPTER: 60

2

PASSING TIME

Nothing is more familiar than the passage of time. "Seize the day!" they say, because "What's here today is gone tomorrow." But while it admittedly *seems* to us that time moves along, it's just not clear how it does so. For time is not a physical object or a thing: it doesn't exist first in one place, then in another. But then in what sense, exactly, does it really move?

Indeed if it were truly moving we ought to be able to say how quickly. You may think that clocks measure that rate, but actually that's not quite right.

What a clock measures, in fact, is not time but rather how some physical things are correlated with other physical things. You glance at the clock and see that it reads 1:13 p.m., and then glance again and see 1:15 p.m. Those two glances are correlated with those two readings, apparently measuring two minutes of time. But now imagine that between those glances everything in the universe sped up together, including your brain activity and thoughts and sensations and the mechanisms of the clock. Those two glances would still be correlated with those two readings, but less than two minutes would have passed—and you'd never notice the difference. So the clock isn't actually measuring the time itself!

If we're really to imagine time itself moving, distinct from all physical things, we must imagine the universe to be entirely empty of all physical things and ask ourselves whether time would still flow. Again, it's tempting to say yes. But then remember that it's an *empty* universe: there is nothing in it. But if there is truly nothing in it, then nothing can be happening, nothing can be occurring, and nothing can really be moving.

"Time flies", they also say, "when you're having fun." I'm all in favor of having fun. But having fun won't pass the time more quickly, if time doesn't really pass at all.

RELATED CHAPTER: 40

3

THE WOMAN OF MY DREAMS

We all know that experience: some exquisite, beautiful dream, into which the alarm clock suddenly and rudely intrudes. We wake up, and our day begins.

Or does it?

Can you in fact be sure that you're not dreaming right now—that you haven't been dreaming your entire life? This is not merely a sleepy philosophers' question. For if you can't be sure you haven't been dreaming, then how can you be sure that *anything* you believe about the world is true?

Could you pinch yourself? Well, you could. But then how would you know that you didn't just dream the pinch itself and then transition into a different dream?

Indeed I once decided to keep a log of my dreams. I quickly found that on waking I couldn't remember the dreams I'd had earlier in the night, so I started waking up during the night to write them down. A few nights of this interrupted sleep and I was exhausted! So my body (or mind) got the better of me: I woke up one morning to discover that my notebook was actually empty. I had only *dreamed* I had woken up to write down my dreams!

At that point I knew I was defeated. But I also knew I had a deep problem. I am positive, right now, 100%, that I am awake and writing this. I'm also positive, right now, 100%, that I have a wife, that I have a physical body, and that other physical objects exist, because I perceive all these things. But then again I was equally positive during my failed experiment that I was awake and writing down dreams. And look how far that got me.

Could it be, then, that nearly everything I believe about the world is false? That even my lovely, lovely wife is only literally the woman of my dreams?

RELATED CHAPTERS: 30, 42, 52, 56

4

MY MIND IS ELSEWHERE

You can't deny that your mind exists. After all, the very act of denying requires the ability to form thoughts, which seems to be a *mental* ability—so denying that you have a mind would amount to proving that you do! What's unclear, however, is just what it *means* to have a mind. We know that we have brains, which are purely physical objects. The question is whether our minds just *are* our brains. And important differences between the mental and physical suggest that they are not.

For example, ordinary physical things have spatial properties: they take up space, they have sizes, shapes, locations, etc. But the mind does not seem to be spatial. It doesn't make sense to ask how "big" that thought is, or what the shape of your consciousness is. Nor does it make sense to ask *where* a thought or perception might be located. If you were to shrink down inside a brain, all you'd see would be lots of molecules zipping about.

You would never find a "thought" or "perception"——since they are not literally located anywhere in the brain.

Minds also have a unique feature: their owners have a special access to them. You can directly know what you are thinking in a way no one else can know what you are thinking. But no physical objects have this feature. Since physical objects all exist in space we all have equal access to them, even to each other's brains. In fact, doctors have even greater access to what's going on in your brain than you do, by means of medical imaging! But simply looking into your brain will never allow them to feel whatever you are feeling. That belongs to you alone in a way your body and brain do not.

It's not clear exactly what a mind is, unfortunately. But it is clear that the only thing in the head is the brain, and that the mind, in the deepest of senses, is elsewhere.

RELATED CHAPTERS: 9, 13, 16, 19, 22, 24, 30, 31, 42, 48, 52, 55, 56, 57

5

DO THE RIGHT THING

If only we knew what that was. Or rather, if only we knew how we knew what that was.

Consider an action such as feeding a helpless hungry child. Everyone agrees that that is a morally good thing to do. But now if you were to witness someone doing this, what would you see? You'd see the person feeding and the child fed; you'd see the food, the chewing, perhaps you'd see the child smile. But here's something you wouldn't see: the actual goodness of the action. "Goodness" is not the kind of property which is literally visible.

Our eyes see only light and color, after all. But good and bad and right and wrong are not equivalent to light or color so of course our eyes can't see them. And more importantly, what our eyes see at best is how things actually are at a given moment. But moral properties are about how things *ought* to be. To say that feeding a hungry child is good is to say that one *ought* to do it. And our eyes are just not equipped for seeing that sort of thing.

It's easy to overlook this fact since we reach our moral judgments so quickly. If you witnessed a murder you'd be so immediately aware of its wrongness that you wouldn't realize that its wrongness is not something you can actually see. But now you might wonder: if you don't know about whether an action is right or wrong by your senses, then how *do* you know it?

So you might be pretty confident you know which actions are right and wrong. Feed that hungry child; be kind; don't steal donuts. You might even be confident in your moral beliefs about more controversial issues. But unless you can say a little more about *how* you know what rightness and wrongness are, you ought not be so confident about what it is you're confident about.

RELATED CHAPTERS: 12, 20, 23, 26, 29, 39, 45, 49, 54, 57, 58, 59

6

PUTTING INTO WORDS WHAT GOES WITHOUT SAYING

Language is as important to human beings as it is mysterious.

You make some sounds and people somehow respond appropriately. But of course only certain sounds, namely the meaningful ones, such as words. And only certain people, namely those who understand your language, who grasp the meanings of your words. So if we want to understand language, we must know more about what "meaning" is.

The first surprising result is that meaning is abstract. That means that it isn't a physical thing and it doesn't exist anywhere in space. Someone has just uttered the word "dog," let's say. The word itself is a physical object, a sound, some vibrating air molecules. A physicist could discover every physical property of that object: its location, its motion, its frequency, etc. But its *meaning* won't be found amongst those properties. The sound may *convey* a meaning, but its meaning is not literally found with or inside the sound.

Similarly, the reason you may not understand Chinese is *not* that your ears aren't working properly. Rather it's because ears only detect physical objects such as sounds, and meanings aren't physical objects. You could have the finest ears around and you'll still stare blankly when someone addresses you in Chinese.

But there's another surprising result.

Consider these two sentences: "It is raining" and "*Il pleut.*" If you know French then you know that these sentences have the same meaning. But now what language is the *meaning* in, so to speak? It isn't in English because then the French sentence would lack it; nor vice versa. So the meaning itself is in *no language at all*.

Understanding a language thus somehow requires us to grasp abstract things that are not detectable by our senses and which are independent of language altogether.

It's a good thing it's much easier to do than to say how it is done!

RELATED CHAPTERS: 15, 25, 35, 47, 55

7

GOD'S ODDS

You're playing poker with friends. Your buddy Fred draws the Ace, King, Queen, Jack, and Ten of spades—a Royal Flush, the highest ranking standard poker hand—the odds against which are roughly 650,000 to 1. Lucky Fred! In the next hand he draws those five cards again. OK that's unusual, but hey, you've known each other since childhood. But then he draws them again, and again. Yes you were best man at each other's weddings but that doesn't suppress your homicidal feelings. When he draws them yet again you find yourself reaching for a weapon.

When something incredibly unlikely occurs, it's very difficult to believe it occurs by chance. Fred is obviously cheating. He will plead that he isn't, even as you beat your lifetime of shared memories out of him. But it's nearly impossible to believe.

But now consider. There are some basic physical properties of the universe, such as the charge of the electron, the precise strength of gravity, the speed of light, etc. Each one could have had any of an infinite number of values. Gravity (for example) could have been slightly stronger, or a lot stronger, or slightly weaker. Had any one of these properties been even *slightly* different, then our universe could not have existed—with its planets and stars and life and us, we conscious, rational, morally aware beings. The odds against all these properties simultaneously having precisely the one value necessary for this universe are quite literally astronomical.

And yet here we are.

If you reached for your piece when Fred got his fifth Royal Flush then perhaps you should be reaching now. For when something incredibly unlikely occurs it is very difficult to believe it occurs by chance. And there is nothing quite as incredibly unlikely as precisely this universe, amongst all the possible universes that might have been.

There would obviously be only one being capable of stacking this deck.

If it's likely that Fred is cheating, then it's all the more likely that God exists and is responsible for this universe.

RELATED CHAPTERS: 17, 26, 36, 43, 57, 59

8

EVERYTHING THAT EXISTS

If we're going to think about things, then we need to think about just which things there are to think about. So let's try to make a list of everything that exists—starting with the questions which arise immediately as one sets out to construct such a list.

Let's start simply, with some ordinary physical things. You might want to list trees, say. But there are many different kinds of trees. Is merely listing "trees," and thus leaving out all those differences, to leave something crucial off the list? On the one hand, no; "trees" covers all trees. But on the other hand, that there are different kinds of trees is a significant fact about the world, one which seems necessary for our list to be comprehensive, which a list of "everything" should be! And then what about forests—are these redundant once we've listed the trees? On the one hand, again, a world with scattered trees is different from one where they're collected into forests; but on the other, what exactly is a forest over and above its trees? Wouldn't it be redundant to list the trees *and* the forests? But then by the same reasoning, what is a tree over and above its atoms? Perhaps we should just list the basic particles that physicists tell us compose the world, or perhaps just "matter." Or again, would leaving off the list the different collections of matter into objects be to leave our list, of *everything*, somehow incomplete?

And what exactly is an object, anyway? We often speak about an object by listing its properties. We say of an apple that it is round and red. So should we say that the apple, the object, is somehow distinct from those properties since "it" has "them"? And if so, does the apple deserve a separate line on our list from the roundness and redness? But then again, what is the apple once you take away its roundness, redness, etc.?

Our list of everything, regretfully, does not yet include itself.

RELATED CHAPTERS: 22, 28, 31, 32, 40, 41, 50, 51, 52

9

TRUE COLORS

I'm a terrible dresser—but my dressing problem is not *entirely* my fault. My shirt and sweater today in fact matched perfectly in my walk-in closet , but then in front of my class they suddenly didn't match at all. I could solve the practical problem by holding my class in my closet. But that wouldn't solve the philosophical problem.

What color is this shirt in my closet, anyhow? I'll say blue. I'll still call it blue outside at noon on a sunny spring day in New York, even though it looks a slightly different color here than in the closet. And I'll still call it blue under the fluorescent lights of my classroom though it now looks nothing like the sweater that matched its color in my closet. But using the same word can't mask the fact that this shirt keeps changing colors on me.

Or does it? Nothing about the shirt has changed. How can it have changed colors when *it* hasn't changed at all?

Maybe I should just say that it *appears* different colors to me. But now if it appears to change colors when it really hasn't, then some of my perceptions must be wrong. But which ones? Perhaps my dimly lit closet is not the "true" viewing context, but it's not obvious that natural sunlight is any better. After all, the sun on a spring noon in New York produces quite a different color from the sun on a wintry late afternoon in London, so which sunlight is the "true" one? And why not say that fluorescent light *improves* on sunlight, and that *it* lets us see the true color?

Maybe we should drop the idea that physical objects have a "true" color altogether. That way we don't have to decide which light gives us the true color, because there is none. Rather we can say that objects have every color they appear to have, in their different contexts. So my shirt does not have *a* true color—only true color*s*.

Now everybody out of this closet.

RELATED CHAPTERS: 4, 16, 30, 42, 52

10

THERE IS NO PATH NOT TAKEN

Every choice I make seems to present two options: the one I choose, and the one I instantly regret not having chosen. I find myself wishing for a "do-over," as if I could roll back time and make the other choice. But of course you can't do that. Even if you could roll back time you couldn't make the other choice.

For what explains the choices we make? Well, lots of things. Sometimes we have hunches and instincts. We have complicated features such as our personality and character. Many of our choices are brought about by our particular beliefs and desires, or values. And there are the laws of nature. We are at least physical creatures and our bodies and brains operate according to those laws. And what *we* do next is pretty much what our brains tell us to do.

But now, do we control any of these things?

Certainly not our hunches; these just happen to us.

Certainly not our personality: if nerdy people could, wouldn't they become cool, like us? Can we control what we believe? Just try to believe that there's an elephant directly in front of you. You can't do it. Your values? Just try to switch your opinion on some current moral controversy. You can't. And we certainly don't control the laws of nature controlling our brains.

We don't control *any* of the factors which control our behavior.

Living life forward it often feels like we have genuine options before us; that the road forks, and it's up to us which path to take. But that is an illusion. There are no forks. What you "choose" is entirely determined by all these factors out of your control. In fact there's just a single road ahead, stretching on with all its twists and turns, and you've simply got no choice but to follow it.

RELATED CHAPTERS: 23, 34, 43, 53

11

THE ONE THING I KNOW IS THAT I KNOW NOTHING

Falser words have rarely been spoken. But it's not because Socrates—their famous utterer—knew plenty, but because it's doubtful that he *knew* that he knew nothing. For knowing *that* would require an understanding of what knowing is, in order to be sure that one lacked it. And that's one thing that we don't yet seem to have.

For sometimes what we know are facts or sentences: Fred knows that there was a French Revolution. Other times it's more like a skill or an ability: Frederique knows how to tie her shoes. Other times it's more like an experience: you don't know what sushi tastes like until you taste Harushi's sushi. But is there anything these share, by virtue of which they all count as examples of "knowing"?

One might suggest that having a skill, or knowing what

sushi tastes like, just amounts to knowing a set of facts or sentences. But it is almost impossible to express most skills in sentences at all. When you teach your child to tie her shoes you inevitably do it by *demonstrating* it, precisely because you don't have the words. I once had a jazz piano teacher who explained how to improvise: "There are twelve tones, man. You just gotta get into it." No wonder I stink at the piano.

And even if we could express various skills in sentences, simply "knowing" the sentences wouldn't give you the skill. If it did there'd be no need for golf pros—you could just read a good golf book, then beat Tiger Woods.

Nor do experiences reduce to knowing sentences. Knowing what Harushi's sushi tastes like doesn't allow you to put it into words, food critics notwithstanding. Indeed even animals could know what it tastes like, and they lack language abilities altogether.

So we've got all these different things, and there is nothing they share by virtue of which they all count as "knowing." Despite everything we may take ourselves to know, then, we just don't know exactly what it means to say that we know them.

RELATED CHAPTERS: 14, 19, 27, 30, 33, 38, 44, 46, 56, 57

12

DON'T WORRY, BE HAPPY—UNLESS WORRYING MAKES YOU HAPPY

There's plenty of moral controversy, to be sure. But there's also a lot of moral agreement. Make quick lists of some actions you think of as uncontroversially morally good ones and morally bad ones and ask a friend to do the same. You and your friend will probably find much overlap in your two lists. In fact it's easy to generate lists that most people more or less agree with.

What's harder is explaining just why that's so easy.

The lists just can't be arbitrary. There must be something that all good actions have in common by virtue of which they *count* as good and something else that all bad actions have in common. Well here's one idea: the moral value of an action is determined by how much overall happiness the action produces. Morally good actions maximize that happiness, while bad ones fail to.

Treating happiness as the fundamental moral value makes a lot of sense. Suppose you ask your friend why he chose to go to a certain college. He might say: because that college will help him get a good job. And why does he want that? Because he wants a nice home and to buy lots of nice things. And why those? Eventually he will say: because that will make me happy. If you then ask him why he wants to be happy he will stare at you like you're crazy. That's because everything we want, we want for the sake of the happiness it brings us; but happiness we want for its own sake.

Happiness is the fundamental thing we value.

Some may object by insisting that morality must ultimately be traced back to God. But our theory is perfectly happy (so to speak) with doing that, if you happen to believe in God. For presumably a benevolent God would want human beings to be happy, so whatever morality God provides would increase human happiness.

If it didn't, then *that* would truly be something to worry about.

RELATED CHAPTERS: 5, 20, 26, 39, 45, 54, 57

13

MENTAL BILLIARDS

Nothing is more familiar than the causal interaction between our minds and our bodies. Light travels from this page into your eyes, jiggles your physical brain, and then you have a mental perception, namely the visual experience of this page before you. Or you have some thoughts in your mind about this book—such as "I must tell all my friends about it immediately!"—and then your physical arm starts moving towards the telephone.

How familiar; and how mysterious.

For minds and bodies seem to be very different sorts of entities. For example, physical things (like our brains) have spatial properties while mental things do not. And how can there possibly be causal interactions between spatial and non-spatial things?

After all, ordinary physical things exert causal influence by contact or collision. One moving billiard ball collides with a second and sets it in motion. But the mind, not being spatial in nature, could never literally make contact or collide with anything physical. So how exactly can mental events cause physical ones and vice versa? How can brain jiggles cause mental perceptions and mental thoughts cause physical arms to pick up the phone, if literally neither can make contact with the other?

There's another problem. The brain is a physical object undergoing a sequence of physical events. As far as science can tell, the laws of physics govern all physical activities including these. But then the complete causal story about why your arm moves can be told in terms of brain jiggles and muscle contractions. Yes you desire to tell your friends about this book and your arm moves—but what causes your arm to move is your brain jiggling, not your desire! But then what did your mind, your thoughts, have to do with anything? The mind seems unable to cause or do *anything* in a world which seems completely explainable by physics.

Quite mysterious.

Now about those phone calls?

RELATED CHAPTERS: 4, 18, 37

14

THE RATIONAL THING TO DO IS TO ACT IRRATIONALLY

There are two boxes. You may choose Box 2 alone or both boxes. Box 1 contains $100. Box 2 contains either zero or a million dollars, depending on what a certain "Predictor" has predicted. If she predicted you will take Box 2 alone she put $1M into it. If she predicted you'll take both boxes she left Box 2 empty. The Predictor has done her work and left the room. A billion people have done this experiment before you, and the Predictor has predicted correctly for every one.

What is the rational choice for you to make?

Well, if she has predicted *your* choice correctly, then if you take Box 2 alone she'll have put $1M in it and if you take both boxes she'll have left Box 2 empty, yielding you only the $100 from Box 1. So it seems rational for you to take Box 2 alone.

But on the other hand, right now Box 2 has either zero or

$1M in it. If zero you're better off taking both boxes because at least you'll get Box 1's $100; if $1M then again you're better off taking both boxes because you'll get the $1M *plus* the $100. So either way you're better off taking both boxes. So the rational thing to do seems to be to take both boxes!

So which to choose?

While it seems unbelievably improbable, with her track record, that the Predictor will predict wrongly for you, in fact it is not *absolutely* impossible. But the second argument exhausts all the logical possibilities. It is literally impossible for that reasoning to go wrong. And when you must choose between what's unbelievably improbable to go wrong and what's *impossible* to go wrong, you must choose the latter.

So you take both boxes. And for the billionth plus one consecutive time the Predictor predicted correctly and left Box 2 empty. You slink home with your $100, having only the small consolation of knowing that at least you did the rational thing.

Unless the rational thing would have been to act irrationally?

RELATED CHAPTERS: 11, 46

15

A ROSE BY ANOTHER NAME WOULDN'T BE A ROSE

There's a riddle. How many legs does a dog have if you call its tail a "leg"? There are at least three possible answers. Five: its four legs plus its tail, now called a "leg." One: if its tail is called a "leg," it's only got one of *those*. And four: calling the tail a "leg" does not make it one. Which is the best answer? Well, it just doesn't matter. Your answer depends on what you mean by the word "leg," and you're free to attach whatever meaning you like, at least for this riddle.

But what *do* you mean when you use the most straightforward words in language, namely names?

Sometimes we refer to a thing by describing it: "the man who wrote *Hamlet*." Sometimes we refer to that same thing by a name: "Shakespeare." The difference is that the name refers to the thing without actually describing it in any way. This suggests a natural answer to our question: names simply mean the things they refer to.

But now consider the sentence "Santa Claus does not exist." Sad, I know, but true. And if our sentence is true then Santa does not exist, in which case the name "Santa" does not refer to any actual thing. But then by our natural theory the name "Santa," now referring to nothing, would be meaningless, in which case the original sentence would be meaningless. And if the sentence were meaningless it's hard to see how it could be true—which it clearly is.

So we need a better theory.

The meaning of a name must, in other words, be something *other* than the thing it refers to; then "Santa" can perhaps be meaningful even without the jolly old fellow himself. Of course it's hard to say what the meaning of a name could be if it's *not* the thing the name refers to. But at least it's clear that the natural theory does not have a tail to stand on.

RELATED CHAPTERS: 6, 25, 35, 47

16

TWO HANDS IN A BUCKET

My wife and I fight regularly over only one thing: the thermo-stat. I lower it when she's not looking and she raises it when I'm not looking. Recently I took it to the next level. When she was-n't looking I installed a special lock on the thermostat. The next time I wasn't looking she installed a new lock on the front door. Now I walk around the house half-dressed a lot.

Now if only she believed that the room were (say) below seventy degrees Fahrenheit! Then, with a thermometer, I could gleefully demonstrate her error. But unfortunately we both agree that it's seventy degrees. What we disagree about is *whether seventy degrees is warm or cold*. And it's just not clear if either of us can be wrong about that.

Imagine an experiment. Stick one hand in a freezer and the other in a heated oven. Then dunk them both into a bucket of room temperature water. What would you experience? No doubt the freezer hand would feel a warm sensation while the oven hand would feel a cool sensation. But now: is the water *itself* warm or cold?

Well, it can't be both. The very same water cannot be both warm and cool since those are opposite properties. Nor have we any basis to say that it's one over the other. Both hands are sensing equally well, after all; it would be entirely arbitrary to decide that one is correct and the other not.

Rather we should conclude that it's *neither*. Warmth and coolness are not really properties of the water, despite all appearances, but instead only sensations in the perceiver's mind. The water may be seventy degrees Fahrenheit but that temperature is itself neither warm nor cold. We just perceive it that way, and each perception is equally legitimate.

So now maybe my wife can just put on another layer?

RELATED CHAPTERS: 4, 9, 30, 42, 52

17

CAN JESUS MAKE A BURRITO SO HOT HE COULDN'T EAT IT?

Even the cartoon character Homer Simpson (who posed this question) has a philosopher within. And though he is not exactly the paradigm of reverence, the question is a real one for any philosophically reverent person. For one of the first properties that believers ascribe to God is that He is omnipotent or all-powerful, which means at least that there is or could be nothing God cannot do. And here is where Homer's question fits in—or at least a somewhat more reverent version thereof:

Can God create a stone so heavy that He cannot lift it?

There are only two possible answers here: yes or no.

Suppose, first, we say no. But then there is something that God cannot do: create such a stone. And if there's something He cannot do then He is not omnipotent after all.

So suppose we say yes. If God can create such a stone then

there could exist a stone so heavy God could not lift it. But then there could be something God cannot do, namely lift that stone. And if there could be something God cannot do, then again He is not omnipotent after all.

Some try to avoid this conclusion by insisting that God simply never will make the stone, so there never will actually exist the thing He cannot do. But this doesn't work. To be omnipotent, it's not enough that there *happens* to be nothing He cannot do. Rather, there could not even *possibly* be something He cannot do. And if He can create that stone—even if He doesn't—then there *could* be something He cannot do, namely lift it.

Since yes and no are the only possible answers and each leads to the same conclusion, then either way there is no omnipotent being. So if God is supposed to be omnipotent it follows that there is no God.

That's some powerful burrito!

RELATED CHAPTERS: 7, 26, 36, 43, 57, 59

18

SURGEON GENERAL'S WARNING: EVERYTHING CAUSES EVERYTHING

A longtime smoker dies of lung cancer. The family says the smoking caused it; the physician says it was the victim's weak lungs; and the tobacco company (who paid the physician) blames it on everything except the smoking. Who is right?

Well, they all are. And no one is.

Let's take a simple a case: you strike a match and it lights. Most of the time we'd say the striking was the cause of the lighting. But in fact there were many other factors as relevant to the lighting as the striking. For starters, it's obviously crucial that the match was coated with appropriate chemicals, that it was made of a flammable wood, that oxygen was present, and so on. Equally necessary were the physical properties of the surface on which it was struck: had it been struck on butter or on water or on your nose, it would not have lighted. And even more fundamentally, we must include the very laws of physics and chemistry which dictate that when matches so made are so struck etc., a lighting will ensue.

But even *these* are just the beginning. For it was also necessary that no stiff wind was blowing; that no rain was falling and that you were not in the shower; that no earthquake covered the match in debris; and that no other gases antagonistic to lighting were present. So too was it necessary that no other match or lighter or fire-breathing dragon had lit the match before it was struck, that it did not spontaneously disappear at the moment of striking, and that (most generally) God did not intervene with some inconvenient anti-lighting miracle.

In short, we can't simply say that the striking of the match caused its lighting. We ought rather to say that more or less everything existing in the universe caused the lighting, *as well as more or less everything not existing.*

I'm sure the tobacco companies will be happy to hear that the same goes for the lung cancer.

I wonder why they never invite philosophers to testify.

RELATED CHAPTERS: 13, 37

19

SEEING RED

Human beings, as we have seen, are a house divided. On the one hand we are physical bodies; but on the other we have mental features such as consciousness, and thought, and perception. Many insist that the physical facts about us—about our brain and its activities—are ultimately all the facts there are: after all, the mind is admittedly very mysterious, and doesn't seem to fit very well with the operations of our brains so successfully studied by science. And yet we might perhaps resist this insistence.

Imagine that Mary has been raised in an entirely black and white environment. Though her life is quite literally drab she does receive a first rate education, both by black and white textbooks and by lectures on a black and white TV, and she devotes herself to the study of the brain. This is far in the future of course, so by this time brain science is perfectly complete.

Mary thus comes to know every physical fact there is to know about how the brain and its related systems operate: how brain cells work, how they're connected to sensory organs such as the eyes, what happens when the eyeball is stimulated by light, etc. She knows literally everything physical there is to know about what the brain does when (for example) someone sees colors, such as red. Of course she herself has never had that experience, although she knows precisely how her brain would respond if she did.

One day it happens. Mary is released from her room, and boy does she see red when she sees red for the first time. Damn them for depriving me of this! she exclaims. It's *gorgeous*! Mary, at last, has learned something: what red looks like, or what it's like to see red.

But wait: if she already knew everything physical about perception and yet she learns something—then this new fact she learns must not be a physical fact.

Mysterious as it may be, there's more to us, then, than the purely physical.

RELATED CHAPTERS: 4, 11, 22, 48, 50

20

YOU CHOOSE, YOU LOSE

You notice five children playing on some railroad tracks. Absorbed in their play, they don't notice the train coming down the track towards them. But luckily, the track forks before them and you are standing right at the switch. By merely pressing the button you can divert the train and thereby spare the children. But then you notice that down the other track is a single child playing alone. To do nothing is to allow the train to kill the five children on the first track; to press the button is to save those five but send the solitary child to her destiny. What should you do?

To many people it's as obvious as it is unpleasant that you must press the button: the right thing to do is to kill the one in order to save the many.

But now consider a different scenario. You are a doctor in a pediatric emergency ward. Five children are about to die from different failing organs: heart, kidney, lung, etc. You notice that outside, playing in the hospital playground, is a single healthy child playing alone. You happen to know that she has the same blood type as all the dying children. Technology has improved so much that it would be a relatively simple matter to snatch the playground child, harvest her organs, and transplant them into the respective dying children, thereby saving them all. For you to do nothing is to allow the five children to die; to give the word is to save those five but send the solitary child to her destiny. What should you do?

To many people it's now as unpleasant as it is obvious that you must *not* press the button: the right thing to do is to spare the one and kill the many.

But the two situations seem fundamentally analogous. So are people's moral beliefs deeply confused here? Or is it that morality itself, perhaps, is confused—that whichever way you choose, you lose?

RELATED CHAPTERS: 5, 12, 39, 54

21

REALLY MOVED, BY THE UNREAL

I'm a weeper. I rarely make it through a decent book or movie without the tears flowing. I bawl when Jimmy Stewart begs Clarence, in *It's a Wonderful Life*, to let him live again. In the cinema I could not suppress an embarrassingly loud sob when the Beast, astonished, murmurs to the Beauty, "You came back, Belle; you came back." And Bogart putting Bergman on that *Casablanca* plane? Always good for at least three hankies.

What I don't understand is why. Why am I moved when the joys and sorrows in fact are not my own—nor even real?

One idea is that when immersed in a movie we temporarily forget that we're observing a fiction. But that seems hard to accept. If I'm watching a DVD I may well get up, make a phone call, then resume watching and weeping. Or I might continue munching popcorn right through my tears. I certainly wouldn't do those things during some real-life sorrow. And similarly

I might feel terror when watching *Jurassic Park*—yet I'm never tempted to run screaming from the cinema, which I surely would do should I even briefly forget that those raptors aren't real.

Another idea is that we are moved out of empathy or compassion. After all, I rarely make it through the evening news without weeping at the misery, either. Yet even so, it seems, the question remains. The pain I learn about this way is not *my* pain. The awful events reported did not happen to me, nor, typically, have I even experienced anything very similar in my own life. To say I have empathy is to say that I *am* moved. But it is not to explain *why* I am moved.

And surely not to explain why I am moved by things which aren't real.

So no, nobody is really put on a plane when Bogart puts Bergman on that plane; and nobody really comes back when Belle the Beauty comes back. But for some reason that doesn't stop me from really reaching for yet another box of Kleenex.

22

YOU ARE NOT WHAT YOU EAT

Take a bite of that burger. What are now entering your body are various atoms such as hydrogen, oxygen, carbon, etc. Most of these, it turns out, were originally created inside distant stars which then exploded and scattered across the cosmos. So what's now becoming you originally arose inside a star. (Your mother always *said* you were stellar; for once she was right.)

But wait: becoming who, exactly?

You are what you eat, people say. The idea is presumably that you are just the molecules which make up your body. Only here's the problem. Those molecules are constantly changing. At every moment, you are exhaling and sweating and shedding lots of molecules, and inhaling and ingesting others. But if you are the same person who started reading this chapter a moment ago while your molecules are not the same, then you can't just be your molecules.

In fact, every molecule in your body is replaced approximately every seven years. If you are just your molecules then you are not merely a *somewhat* different person than you were seven years ago, you are a *totally* different person. On the plus side you can truly dissociate yourself from that loser you were back in school; but on the down side, it's no longer obvious why you should be entitled to cash *his* savings bonds.

Imagine now that the molecules constituting you seven years ago were to be recollected and reassembled. If you are just your molecules then that collection is also you, if a younger version. But then there would be two yous, which certainly seems odd—at least as odd as the argument you two would have over who owns those savings bonds.

I personally am an awful eater. Forget whole grain—I'll take parts. There's nothing which doesn't taste better to me with sugar, including sugar. The philosopher in me is not sure exactly who or what I am, but he can at least take comfort in knowing that we are not what we eat.

RELATED CHAPTERS: 4, 8, 19, 32, 41, 50, 57

23

THE DEVIL MADE ME DO IT

In the beginning was the excuse. Adam blamed Eve, she blamed the snake, and the rest is human history. The Devil is particularly prominent here, of course, since he loves making people misbehave. He also works in subtle (i.e. not disprovable) ways—very conveniently for the blame-shifting evil-doer.

Now, implicit in all this is the idea that if you are made to do something then you are not morally responsible for it. And implicit *there* is the idea that if you are unable to do otherwise than you do, then you are not morally responsible for doing it. Since the Devil presumably takes away your ability to do otherwise—perhaps by tempting you beyond your resistance—he also takes away your moral responsibility.

But is this principle really true? Could you be morally responsible for doing something even *if* you could not have done otherwise?

Imagine that Fred is contemplating murdering Frederique. That's a *really* evil deed, so the Devil decides to ensure that Fred will do it. He listens in on Fred's thoughts. If Fred is about to decide to murder, the Devil will do nothing. But if he observes Fred deciding against murder then he will fiddle with Fred's brain to change Fred's mind. Fred is therefore unable to do otherwise than to terminate Frederique: the Devil will either act or not, and either way Frederique's a goner.

Suppose now that Fred's deliberations conclude as the Devil wanted: goodbye Frederique. The Devil never intervenes. We'd obviously hold Fred morally responsible for this action. After all he decided on his own to do it, with no intervention by anybody else. And yet it remains true that he was unable to do otherwise. So we have here a case where someone is morally responsible for an action even if he couldn't do otherwise. Which means that the general principle above must be incorrect.

But then why should someone making you do something *ever* free you of responsibility for it?

RELATED CHAPTERS: 5, 10, 34, 43, 53

24

CYBER-ROMANCE

I met my wife online. The philosopher in me was matched to the philosopher in her and the rest followed logically, as they say. I wanted to thank the program that brought us together, but was disappointed when the florist refused my order. Programs aren't people, he insisted. They don't want your flowers.

So unenlightened!

Could a computer be programmed to be a person, genuinely to have a mind? To determine that, we must know exactly what minds are. But all we have to go on there is our conscious awareness of our own minds, and we never have that kind of access to anyone else's "inner" mental life. So how could we ever decide if (say) *Star Wars'* R2D2 is one of us—or just a complicated impersonal thing, like a thermostat?

There's only one way: by observing its behavior. So suppose

a computer, connected to a robotic body, could navigate through a cluttered room, carry on a conversation, and display common sense in its behavior. Suppose a computer robot behaved such that you couldn't detect *any* difference between its behavior and that of an ordinary person's. Should you say that such a computer is a person?

It's tempting to say no, that it only *seems* to have a mind. But if you deny a mind to such a computer then shouldn't you do the same to other human beings? For what makes you think that they have minds other than the fact that they behave as if they do?

In fact people really are just complex programs already, running on the hardware of the brain. If my wife turned out to have a lot of circuits inside, why should that matter? She'd still be a whiz at calculating tips, fixing my spelling, and finding cheap airfares. And her beautiful deep brown optical detectors would still light up every time I brought home flowers.

And that's good enough for me.

RELATED CHAPTERS: 4, 55

25

"IT DEPENDS ON WHAT THE MEANING OF THE WORD 'IS' IS"

Philosophers, lawyers, spin doctors—and the former U. S. President who infamously uttered the sentence above to a grand jury—all suffer from a bad reputation: they play games with words. That may well be true, but we shouldn't blame the philosopher in a person for those offenses. We should blame the English language for making those offenses possible in the first place.

For English, like other languages, is a mess: it's vague, ambiguous, and inconsistent. And it is most notoriously unclear with respect to one of its most basic words: "is." Sometimes (for example) "is" indicates the present tense: "Fred is eating now." But other times it indicates the future: "Fred is coming later." And other times it is used timelessly: "The number 3 is odd," or "'Is,' simply, is a mess."

And even if we restrict ourselves to the present tense, "is" is no better. For consider the following sentences:

Fred is red
Fred is lead
Fred is Ted
Fred is

To say that Fred is red is to say that redness is one of his properties. (Maybe he's blushing.)

But to say that Fred is lead is to say that he is composed of lead—maybe "Fred" is the name of a statue—in a way we'd never say that blushing Fred is "composed of" redness.

When we say that Fred is Ted we're *identifying* Fred with Ted: Fred and Ted are one and the same person. (Perhaps he's been two-timing some women by using different names.) But we don't say that Fred the statue is "identical" to lead. After all there's plenty of lead in the world that's not affiliated with Fred.

Finally, when we say "Fred is," we're not saying anything about his properties, what he's composed of, or what he's identical to. We're merely saying that he exists.

So "is" *is* a very difficult word. So don't blame the philosophers, the lawyers, the spin doctors, or the former U. S. President (who may be all of the above)—it's English itself which deserves to be impeached.

RELATED CHAPTERS: 6, 15, 35, 47

26

GOD'S TOP TEN

If you believe in God then you probably believe that God created everything. If you believe in morality then you believe that
certain actions are morally right and others wrong. So if you
believe in both God and morality, then you probably believe
that God created morality.

But not so fast.

Let's assume that God's "creation of morality" may be rep-
resented by His dictation of the famous Ten Commandments.
And now ask: did God dictate these commandments
because those things are what's right and wrong to do, or are
those things right and wrong simply because God dictated
them?

Suppose it's the former: God said do it because it's the right
thing to do. But then the commanding comes *after* the rightness
of the action; it is not what *makes* the action right. The action is

already right on its own and God merely informs us about it. So on this view God has not in fact *created* morality.

So suppose we go for the other option: honoring your parents (say) is the right thing to do simply because God tells you to do it. Here the rightness *is* due to God, as God's decreeing it is what *makes* it the right thing to do. Only now we have no explanation for *why* God told us to do this thing as opposed to its opposite. God is a free agent after all and could just as easily have said: "Thou shalt *dishonor* your parents." Was it simply arbitrary or random that God commanded us to honor rather than dishonor?

No. Genuine morality is not arbitrary in this way. There must be a reason that God commands honoring and forbids murdering (say), rather than their opposites. And the reason is that honoring and murdering are already right and wrong, before His commanding. We're back in the first option, in other words—according to which morality is not created by God.

So if you believe in morality you cannot believe that God created everything.

RELATED CHAPTERS: 5, 7, 12, 17, 36, 43, 57, 59

27

THE PROOF IS IN THE (VANILLA) PUDDING

I simply love vanilla pudding. But the philosopher in me loves proving things even more. And unfortunately the former is a lot easier to obtain than the latter.

For what constitutes a "proof" of something? One possible model might come from science. The scientist has a certain theory; according to that theory, if she runs a certain experiment she will get a particular outcome. She then runs the experiment. If she gets the outcome the theory is proved. If not, it is disproved.

But it's not so simple.

In fact all sorts of ultimately false theories have stuck around for years because many of their predictions happened to come true. So simply getting the outcome you expect provides no actual "proof" of your theory. Nor does an unexpected outcome actually *disprove* your theory. For you may have calculated the prediction wrongly; something might have been wrong with your apparatus; or unknown factors might be interfering with your result.

So no experiment can *prove* anything. What we might say instead is merely that various experiments can provide some *evidence* for or against a theory.

But even that doesn't get us all the way.

Suppose you had the theory that "all ravens are black." Obviously the more black ravens you observed the more confident you'd feel about the theory; and if you saw a non-black raven you'd probably give the theory up. But now saying that "all ravens are black" is actually equivalent, if you think about it for a moment, to saying that "all non-black things are not ravens." And if these are equivalent, then any evidence for one must also be evidence for the other.

So here comes the pudding and the problem. If a black raven provides evidence that "all ravens are black," then a non-black non-raven—which vanilla pudding is—would provide evidence that "all non-black things are not ravens." But since those two sentences are equivalent, evidence for one is evidence for the other—so vanilla pudding ends up counting as evidence that "all ravens are black"!

Something has gone wrong somewhere.

RELATED CHAPTERS: 11, 38, 44

28

THERE'S MORE TO THE WORLD
THAN WHAT THERE IS

Sounds pretty paradoxical. But of course by now we know what the philosopher within will say: it is and it isn't.

What there is, is what's actual. What's actual is everything that exists. At the time of writing, I exist, London exists, the number 3 exists, and lots more. But now not all actual things are alike. Yes, you exist as you read this—but you didn't *have* to exist, since there are many possible circumstances in which you *wouldn't* have. Suppose the Big Bang had never occurred; suppose life on Earth had never arisen; suppose your mother *hadn't* hiccupped precisely at the moment of insemination. These things didn't happen but *could* have, and had they, you *wouldn't* have. And that means that your existence is "contingent," i.e. contingent on all the things which brought you about but didn't have to.

To the contrary, consider mathematical objects like the number 3. It was never created; it didn't come into existence by being conceived or born or made, and there are no possible circumstances in which it wouldn't have existed. So the number 3 exists not contingently but *necessarily*.

The actual, then, divides into the contingent and the necessary. But there's more—for not everything is actual.

What makes your existence contingent is that there are possible circumstances in which you wouldn't have existed, and perhaps other things would have existed in your place. (Think of that hiccup!) But if there really are other possibilities, then the world contains more than what is actual. *It must also contain these possibilities*.

Think of it as follows. If you merely listed everything that actually exists you wouldn't have given a complete account of the world—for that list leaves off the true fact about the world that other things *could have* existed. And that's what we mean when we say that the world also contains these possibilities.

So no, there's no more in the world than what there is, if what there is is everything actual *and* possible. But there is more to the world than merely what's actual.

RELATED CHAPTER: 8

29

IT'S ALL RELATIVE

Philosophers frequently disagree. But even normal people have trouble reaching agreement. Think about all the nations at war, the litigation in courts, the children arguing over what game to play. Not surprisingly, it's no different with respect to morality.

There are tremendous moral differences across the world. In various cultures it is morally right to arrange marriages, to suppress political dissent for group harmony, to assign women lesser status than men; in the West these are all wrong. In some cultures it is even a moral obligation to circumcise daughters, while the label "female genital mutilation" pretty much tells you how Westerners feel about the practice. At the same time, many aspects of Western culture are seen as morally objectionable elsewhere, whether it's the materialism and consumerism, the stress on individual self-interest, the immodest modes of dress, and so on.

What shall we make of these differences? Is there any way to determine, in the face of such widespread moral disagreements, who is right and who is wrong?

As far as one of the philosophers in me can see, morality isn't out there in the world in the way that scientific or mathematical facts are. These latter exist independently of human beings and are thus things we need to discover; consequently, all cultures agree about them. Morality, to the contrary, is not something discovered but something invented, by different groups at different times and places. And as with any invention, it's entirely up to the inventor to decide what goes in and what stays out. Thus different cultures can establish whatever moral rules they like, and each culture is the only judge of what is right and wrong within that culture. By the same token, no one is in a position to judge other cultures' moralities.

So who's to say, then, who's right and who's wrong when cultures disagree on morality? Everyone and no one: for everyone can pronounce on their own culture's morals, but nobody can pronounce on another's.

RELATED CHAPTERS: 5, 12, 54, 58

30

WHAT YOU SEE IS NOT WHAT YOU GET

People regularly tell me to come to my senses, but the philosopher in me thinks we should run as far from our senses as we can.

To concentrate just on vision, our eyes deceive us all the time. A square tower may look round from a distance. Our bed sheets look spotless yet harbor more hungry dust mites than we want to know. The moon looks larger on the horizon than above us and yet it isn't. A straight stick in water looks bent. The sky looks blue when in fact it consists only of gas molecules which aren't themselves blue. Objects seem to move across the movie screen when all we're actually seeing is a rapid sequence of still pictures. And that dining room table we paid a month's salary for, for what looks like its solid cherry surface? In fact it's composed mostly of the empty space inside its atoms. Suckers!

Indeed the whole idea that our eyes can tell us how things really are doesn't make a lot of sense. Our perceptions are constantly varying, for one thing, without our having any basis for choosing one perception to be the "true" one. In fact (for example) I shouldn't have suggested above that the stick "really is" straight since even that information only comes from other conflicting perceptions. Instead we should just say that to our visual perception the stick *looks* crooked while to our tactile perception of it under the water it *feels* straight. There is no way of saying how things "really" are. We can only say how things appear to us in different circumstances.

Even more importantly, to tell that our visual perception of a thing is accurate we'd have to compare that perception with the thing itself. But how can we do *that*? Every time we look at the thing we only get another perception of it, and never the thing itself!

Things are simply not, in short, as the eyes have it. So next time you're told to come to your senses—say nay!

RELATED CHAPTERS: 3, 4, 9, 11, 16, 33, 42, 52, 56

31

IT DOESN'T ADD UP

There's a *Sesame Street* episode where the muppet Grover has just mastered adding 1 and 1 to get 2, using blocks. But then oranges are brought out and he begins to weep; he only knows how to add blocks.

This little skit raises some very big questions about numbers.

The humor here relies on our assumption that if you can add blocks, you should be able to add oranges. But why assume that exactly? Because we also assume that numbers are real properties of objects. If the "oneness" of each orange is as real as the "oneness" of each block, then if Grover can grasp one he should be able to grasp the other.

But are objects really intrinsically numbered in this way?

Consider an automobile and ask yourself what number applies to it. Well, it's 1 Jaguar, say. But it's also (say) 4000 components (tires and engine and steering wheel and so on)—and 8 gazillion molecules, and 80 gazillion gazillion atoms, and still a lot more elementary particles. So what number applies to this thing? Think of it as an auto and it's 1; think of it as its components and it's 4000; think of it different ways and different numbers apply. What numbers apply to something depends not just on the thing but on how you choose to *think* about the thing.

Are numbers only in the mind, then? After all, you can know that $1 + 1 = 2$ simply by thinking about it. And further, we are confident of our arithmetic even when the world conflicts with it! Sometimes one cloud runs into another, forming a single larger cloud. So 1 cloud plus 1 cloud yields: 1 cloud. Does this prove that $1 + 1$ does *not* equal 2? Of course not. But *why* not? Because the numbers in our mind don't *really* apply to things like clouds, or any objects in the world at all.

What's surprising, then, is not that Grover couldn't add the oranges—but that he, or any of us, could even add the blocks in the first place.

RELATED CHAPTERS: 4, 8, 56, 57

32

SAME OLD SAME OLD

Your everyday experience is very repetitive: you wake up, you get dressed, you go to work: most days have the "same old" content. But then the fact *that* they are the same is *also* the same each day. So it's the *same old* same old each day.

But wait: in what sense exactly are things the "same" every day?

Yesterday you brushed your teeth: six up and down strokes, six horizontal strokes, etc. Today you do the "same." But these actions differ in many ways: one was on Tuesday the other on Wednesday; in one your strokes were slightly faster than in the other. So why do we consider them the "same"?

In fact how *could* any two things be the "same"? To be the same is to be the same thing; it's for there to be only one thing. The whole idea of *two* things being the "same" doesn't even make any sense!

Or imagine two ketchup bottles exactly the same in every respect. We normally don't hesitate to say here that "those two things are the same." Sameness is everywhere! But again, if sameness means "one," then how can *two* things be the same?

Perhaps the two bottles are the same insofar as they have the same properties: size, shape, color, etc. But that faces the "same" problem. This bottle has this redness, that bottle has that redness; how can their two rednesses be the "same"? Or sometimes we say that the bottles "share" their properties. But two people may share a condo, or a name, or (if conjoined) even a kidney: in each case there is one thing to which both have access. So if the two ketchup bottles share the property of being red, is there literally one thing—"redness"—to which both have access? But how could that be? The two bottles may be separated in space, even miles or continents apart. How could one single thing, one "redness," literally be present in both bottles?

"Sameness" is inconceivable. So in fact every day *is* the same: utterly unique.

RELATED CHAPTERS: 8, 22, 41, 50

33

I CAN'T SEE FOR MILES AND MILES

Indeed you cannot. Not even for kilometers and kilometers, or meters and meters, or feet, or inches. In fact you cannot literally see any distance at all.

Imagine you have your eye on Jessie at the office. It certainly seems that you can see how far away she is from you—ten meters and counting, as Jessie sees you staring and begins to retreat. But all you can "see," strictly speaking, is whatever is available on your retina, the membrane in the back of your eye—which provides the only way for visual information to get inside your brain. The distance between you and Jessie is measured by a straight line from Jessie to your eyeball, namely the line that each light ray travels from her to your eye. And here's the problem: your eye only receives the "end" point of that line. You only receive the light when it hits your retina and your retina simply cannot know how far that light has traveled. So you cannot "see" how far away she is.

Yet Jessie is now fifteen meters away from you and picking up speed.

It gets worse. Again, you see things only by means of the image they cast on your retina. But now the very same retinal image can be cast by objects at almost any distances. For example, you see the moon because it casts an image of a certain size and shape on your retina. But that very same image would be cast there by a very tiny round object very close to your eye, a medium sized object at some distance away, or a great big object such as the moon at a great distance. The retinal image itself therefore carries no information about how far away its object is. And so you simply cannot "see" distance.

Yet there is Jessie now twenty meters away from you frantically dialing the police on a cell phone. How *do* you know this, if not by seeing it?

RELATED CHAPTERS: 11, 30, 56

34

IF YOU READ ONLY ONE BOOK
THIS YEAR ...

Imagine you receive a book entitled *Your Life*. Chapter one starts with your birth and first year of life, and so on, all in impressive detail. Like all good biographies the book contains all and only true statements about your life. But then you notice that the book continues with (hopefully many) chapters on your future.

Suppose (alas) there's some horrible news ahead. The book says that on Saturday night you will get in your car at 8:45 p.m., pick up your beloved at 9:05, then crash at 9:23 at Broad Street and James, killing your beloved. You will obviously try to avoid this outcome. You will not get in the car. But wait—the book contains only true statements. So somehow you must end up in the car. So perhaps you will not drive to your beloved's house. But since the book says you will, your efforts to avoid doing so must fail. How strange! You try to say "Don't get in the car!" But instead you find yourself saying, "Hop in, darling!" You try to avoid the fatal intersection, but again cannot. Some miraculous force compels you to turn the wheel just so, to place you there at 9:23 as that other car runs its red light ...

This story is obviously implausible. It requires invoking mysterious forces compelling you against your will, and nobody believes in such forces. The more plausible thing to believe is simply this: you will be able to avoid the predicted outcomes, any number of ways.

But notice: what generated the whole incredible scenario was the assumption that you could be reliably informed of your future. If what follows from that assumption is something impossible to believe then that assumption must be false. So it's impossible for you to be reliably informed of your future. Nobody—not even God!—could accurately know your future actions and inform you of them.

And why is that? Because for almost any prediction you might be informed of, you could do otherwise.

It's because, in other words, you have free will.

RELATED CHAPTERS: 10, 23, 43, 53

35

BY SHAKESPEARE—OR SOMEONE ELSE OF THE SAME NAME

Like other words names have meanings, and it's natural to think that the meaning of a name just is the thing it refers to. Unfortunately this theory doesn't work, as we saw earlier. So we need another theory.

Consider then how you'd reply if you were asked who you meant by the name "Shakespeare." You'd provide some sort of description, such as "Shakespeare was the author of *Hamlet*." That suggests another rather natural theory: the meaning of a name is the description you associate with the name, and the person referred to by the name is whoever fits that description.

Sounds plausible. But this theory also doesn't work. For if this theory were correct then, strangely, it would be impossible ever to speak falsely about someone!

Suppose you assert that "Shakespeare was the author of *Hamlet*." It's later discovered that that is false; a guy named Marlowe actually wrote *Hamlet*, but Marlowe's authorship got lost to history (conveniently for Shakespeare). Normally we would say here that your original assertion turns out to be a false one about that glory-stealing Shakespeare. But according to our theory the name "Shakespeare" refers to whoever fits the description "the author of *Hamlet*." But then the original sentence was actually about *Marlowe*, since it is he who fits the description! And Marlowe *was* the author of *Hamlet*, so what originally looked like a false sentence about Shakespeare ends up being a true one about Marlowe—someone you've never even heard of!

Something has obviously gone wrong here.

Indeed, something has now gone wrong with two very natural theories about the meaning of names. Perhaps it's time to begin considering something a little more unnatural. I'm sure the author of *Hamlet* would agree—whoever the hell he is.

RELATED CHAPTERS: 6, 15, 25, 47

36

WHY ARE YOU STILL HERE?

Well, I was here a second ago and I haven't left.

Of course when I'm asked this question the asker typically isn't seeking an explanation but rather my immediate departure. But it turns out that that response provides neither.

For the deeper question is this: What keeps you, or anything—this book, this car, this earth—in existence from moment to moment? It certainly seems that any given thing *could*, at least in theory, just go out of existence at any time. So why doesn't it?

Yes, you were here a second ago. But does your existing at one instant explain your existing at the next one? It doesn't seem to. For if it's not impossible for you to go out of existence at any given time, then the fact that you exist at instant 1 doesn't mean that you *must* exist at instant 2. So we still need an explanation why you're still here at instant 2.

It's tempting to say that things have some force or power to endure and *that's* what keeps them in existence. But this answer won't work, because the same problem confronts the force itself! Non-existing things obviously cannot exert any causal powers. So if the force itself doesn't exist at instant 2 then it cannot bring about its effect—such as your existing—at instant 2. So the force itself must endure from instant 1 to instant 2. But what keeps *it* in existence during that interval?

Could some *other* thing, distinct from you, explain why you stay in existence? Not if that other thing could itself go out of existence because then the same problem arises for *it*.

If we're genuinely to explain why we persist from moment to moment, then, it seems we need to invoke the activity of something which could *not* possibly go out of existence.

Could the simple fact that you are here now—and now— and *now*—mean that God exists?

RELATED CHAPTERS: 7, 17, 26, 43, 57, 59

37

SURGEON GENERAL'S RETRACTION: NOTHING CAUSES ANYTHING

Ask two surgeons general, we might say, and you'll get at least two opinions. Previously we saw the opinion that everything causes everything. But that was then.

To return to the familiar example, we say things like this: "the striking of the match caused it to light." What we mean in saying this, in saying that one thing causes another, is that the first event makes or compels the second event to occur. And that means that once the first event occurs the second event *has* to occur: it is *impossible* for the first to occur without the second.

But now are any two events ever actually connected in this way?

To say something is impossible is to say that it involves a contradiction. But there is never any contradiction in the idea of any one distinct event occurring without another. It's easy to conceive (for example) of our match striking but without lighting—you just did! You may be tempted to object: "But given the laws of physics and chemistry, if you strike that match in those conditions it *is* impossible for it not to light!" Well, just imagine the laws of physics being different. No contradiction there either! And if you can conceive of that then you can conceive of the match striking without lighting—in which case it's not impossible to have the first without the second.

So the first does not make or compel the second to occur; it does not, in other words, cause it. Not for the striking and the lighting, and not for any pair of events in the world.

And so the truth of the matter is this: nothing causes anything.

So why, then, do things happen?

RELATED CHAPTERS: 13, 18

38

WILL YOU STILL LOVE ME TOMORROW?

The obvious answer to this question is always yes.

But the not-so-obvious question is how you can ever be *justified* in saying anything about tomorrow, or about the future. Consider your walk to the bus this morning. You were confident that the ground would support every step that you took. But what justified you in believing that your "next" step wouldn't be into a suddenly appearing sinkhole? Past results are surely no *guarantee*, as the small print says, of future performance. But does the earth's fine history of supporting your previous billion steps at least make it *highly likely* that it will support your next step?

It would do so only *if* you assume that the future will be like the past—for if it won't be, then it wouldn't.

But how would you justify that assumption itself?

Well, the future has always been like the past so far. So don't we have reason to believe that it will continue to be like the past? No, for that just repeats the problem. It merely assumes that past patterns will continue to hold into the future. *But that is the very assumption we're trying to justify!* And you can't justify it merely by assuming it's true. Which means that you have no good reason to believe the future will be like the past—or, for that matter, different from it. Which means that past results *don't give you any guide to the future at all.*

So you probably should refrain from saying *anything* about tomorrow. The next time you're asked the title question I would advise you to run—except that you have no good reason to believe that the earth will support your steps. Perhaps you should just silently stay put? Except that, by the same reasoning, you also have no good reason to believe the earth will continue to support you where you are. So maybe the thing to do is as I said: just say yes. And quickly. If you're asked about your hesitation, just say you were contemplating your future together.

RELATED CHAPTERS: 11, 27, 43

39

AN INCONVENIENT TOOTH

There's something about movie popcorn. My sweet tooth I can satisfy anywhere but only movies can satisfy my popcorn tooth. I also firmly believe that you should try to do some good in this world.

And that precisely is the problem.

Think about the roughly $15 you spend whenever you go to the movies. Then think about those commercials you've seen on television: weepy, wide-eyed, hungry children staring at you while you're reminded that just pennies a day could keep that very child from starving to death. You are moved, you resolve—and yet there you are chuckling over Adam Sandler's antics in his latest international blockbuster.

You are spending $15 munching popcorn while children are literally *dying*.

It's easy to rationalize your behavior. "What could my $15 do against the all the world's problems?" Answer: It could save a child's life. "Hey I do plenty of good, I give to charity, donate my time. Can't I just go to the movies?" Answer: You could always do more. Is your evening at the movies worth a child's life? "How can I be sure my $15 will actually do any good?" Answer: Stop going to movies and get involved in the relevant organizations.

In fact it's very hard to justify going to the movies. Or going out to dinner. Or buying new clothes. Or pretty much anything we do. If all of us just cut back a little on our luxuries and redirected our resources we could do an awful lot of good in this world. Take global warming, for example. If everyone who saw Al Gore's *An Inconvenient Truth* had just applied their popcorn money directly towards the problem in some way, perhaps the movie wouldn't have been necessary.

Oh wait—the new Steve Martin movie has just come out!

RELATED CHAPTERS: 5, 12, 20, 49, 54

40

THERE IS NO TIME, LIKE THE PRESENT

I know what time it is. I just don't know what time itself is.

It seems to be composed of past plus present plus future. But the past does not exist—if it did, it would be present! And the future does not *yet* exist, in which case it does not *now* exist. So if time exists, it exists only as the present.

But what is the present?

The present is a moment of no duration. For if it had a duration (a day, an hour, a millisecond, etc.) not all of that duration would be present at once. And while a day is composed of hours and hours of minutes, and so on, the present is not like those temporal intervals: it is not composed of any smaller intervals or parts. For if it were, not all of those parts would be present at once. Rather the present is composed, quite literally, of nothing.

But something composed of nothing must itself be nothing.

Similarly, think about ordinary physical objects. They are all composed of smaller things which in turn are composed of even smaller things. But eventually you reach the bottom level. Today scientists think that the smallest physical objects are things like electrons and quarks and maybe what they call "strings."

But time is not like this. There is no bottom level. No matter how small a temporal interval you are talking about (a microsecond, a nanosecond, etc.), there is always a smaller interval. And if there is no bottom level, there can be no moments of no duration—for such moments clearly would *be* the bottom level, in being indivisible.

The present, in other words, does not exist.

When people say they have no time for something, then, they don't realize how true that is.

For there is no time. Period.

RELATED CHAPTERS: 2, 8, 43, 51

41

MY IDENTITY CRISIS IS HAVING AN IDENTITY CRISIS

It's common on approaching adulthood to experience some sort of identity crisis: Who am I really? What are my deepest principles? Is it really right that my parents continue to support me? When this happened to me, around the age of thirty-five, I became deeply anxious. But then my identity crisis had an identity crisis: what is identity, really? What are its deepest principles? And if not my parents, then who?

Identity is actually a problem for all sorts of things. Is your body identical to the molecules composing it? Are mental states identical to brain states? Is the God of the Old Testament identical to that of the New Testament? If we're to evaluate questions like these, we clearly need some guidance.

So consider the following principle:

"If there's something true of x that's not true of y, then x is not the same thing as y."

This principle makes good sense. But good sense can sometimes lead to nonsense.

Is a statue identical to the clay (say) of which it's composed? It's hard to deny it; there aren't two things there, the statue *and* the clay. But then there are many things true of the one that aren't true of the other. The statue was made by Michelangelo; the clay was made by geological processes. The statue could have been done in marble, but the clay could not have. And the statue is beautiful and priceless while the clay itself is neither.

Somehow, they're not identical!

And think about yourself as of a few moments ago. There's something true of you now that is not true of the earlier you: your awareness of the problem of identity. So the later you is not the same person as the earlier you. Indeed with each passing instant you become one instant older. But then each later you is of a different age than each earlier you so they're not the same person. So with each passing instant one person goes out of existence and another arises.

So who *are* you, exactly?

RELATED CHAPTERS: 8, 22, 32, 50, 57

42

I'LL SEE YOU IN MY DREAMS

"You're crazy; it's all in your mind." The philosopher in me is used to hearing this, usually expressed with a finger pointed towards the door. My typical response is to utter "Exactly!" as the door closes behind me. For it *is* all in the mind.

Imagine the following dream. You're on an island beach, the sun is shining, the ocean is a gorgeous blue, you're sipping a cool margarita with that special someone … And then you wake up. And you're in your bed, at night, in winter, in your apartment, and desperately, desperately alone. We're all familiar with this phenomenon, as we saw earlier: how things appear in our dreams is often not how things really are.

But now this phenomenon is not merely limited to our dreams.

In the dream, at one moment, you gazed at a coconut tree. But consider, now, *what* exactly were you seeing there?

It was not a real—that is, physical—tree, because there is no physical coconut tree in your lonely apartment bedroom. Indeed it was not a physical tree because your eyes were closed: you weren't physically seeing anything at all. You must have been seeing something else: a mental image of a tree, a mental tree. The same goes for everything else in a dream. What we see in dreams, clearly, are just mental images.

Now you are awake. If you are lucky you're reading this book on an island beach, the sun is shining, the ocean is blue . . . Look at a coconut tree. Your visual experience is in every way like your dreamed visual experience of that tree. That's why it's so hard to distinguish dreams from ordinary waking perception. But in a dream what you see are only mental images of objects. So what you see when you look at a tree *even when awake* is but a mental image, and not a real physical tree.

So even awake we never genuinely perceive the physical objects in the world around us.

I'm not crazy: it *is* all in your mind.

RELATED CHAPTERS: 3, 4, 9, 16, 30, 48, 52, 56

43

GOD ONLY KNOWS WHAT YOU'LL DO NEXT

God is supposed to be *omniscient*, to know everything. But then He ought to know what you will do in the future, even if you act freely. But how exactly could God know, right now, what you are going to do freely (say) tomorrow?

Well, there are three ways to acquire knowledge: one may reason about what necessarily must be, one may generalize from past patterns about what will probably be, or one may make observations about what now is.

So suppose God knows the future by the first method: perhaps He knows all the laws of nature, so He calculates what the laws will bring about next and thus knows what you will do tomorrow. That would accommodate His omniscience, to be sure—but only at the cost of your freedom! For if your actions were generated by the laws of nature in this necessary and predictable way then we would hardly say that you acted freely.

So suppose God knows what you'll do tomorrow by the second method: He knows your tastes, preferences, habits, etc., and so combining this information with His own famously accurate weather forecast He predicts what you'll wear tomorrow. This method preserves your freedom: although you may tend to act in patterns it's always open to you not to. The problem rather is that this method is not perfectly reliable: precisely because you're free not to wear the predicted clothing, sometimes you won't. And surely an omniscient God's predictions cannot be less than perfectly reliable!

What about the third way, then, namely observation? There's just one problem: how can God "observe," right now, a future event? You can only observe what exists, and the future doesn't.

So we have a *big* problem. God may know what you will do tomorrow, by method one. Or you may act freely while God uses method two. But we can't have both: that God knows what you will do *and* you do it freely.

RELATED CHAPTERS: 7, 10, 17, 23, 26, 34, 36, 38, 40, 53, 57, 59

44

I'LL TAKE MY CHANCES

If you're a human being (as you probably are), you probably reason about probabilities, at least subconsciously, every second of every day. Whenever you get in your car, light a cigarette, take a step, or hold up a liquor store, you are taking probabilities into account concerning crashes, cancer, sinkholes, or death in a hail of bullets.

But now what exactly do we mean when we say things are "probable" to various degrees? When we say (for example) that "the probability of this coin's landing on heads is 50%"?

Do we mean that if we toss it twice it will land once on heads and once on tails? Clearly not. Perfectly "fair" coins—with a probability of 50% heads—may happen to land heads twice in a row.

Do we mean that if we toss it 100 times it will land precisely 50 times on heads? No again, for a fair coin might perfectly well come out 51–49, or 55–45, or worse, in any 100 particular tosses.

Do we mean that it will *probably* land 50 times (out of 100) on heads? Perhaps, but that wouldn't answer our original question—for if we don't know what it means to say something is 50% probable, we wouldn't know what it means to say it will "probably" land 50 times on heads.

Do we mean that if we were to toss the coin an *infinite* number of times the number of heads will equal the number of tails? One problem here is that at any point where the number of heads equaled the number of tails, the next toss would disturb that ratio—so there will be lots of points at which they are not equal. But that wouldn't take away our claim that there's a 50% probability.

We may think about probabilities all the time. But when we *really* think about them we don't even know what we mean by them. And that is not a good thing.

Probably.

RELATED CHAPTERS: 11, 27

45

SANTA AND SCROOGE

Some people, looking for an inspiring role model, turn to religion and ask themselves, "What would Jesus do?" But it seems to me that Jesus himself probably wouldn't ask that. So what about the next best person: Santa?

Well, generosity is a good thing; I'm not questioning that. But we never learn just why Santa gives, and we cannot morally evaluate him without knowing his motivations. According to some, the actual historical source of the Santa legend originally gave only to the poor. That's admirable, but there's a long way between that and rewarding every little brat on the planet, including the rich ones. And with respect to today's Santa— who rewards those who behave and punishes those who don't—well, if children behave well only to get the latest video game then we're hardly teaching them genuine morality. And if Santa is the key enabler there, so much the worse for Santa.

OK, let's give him the benefit of the doubt. Suppose we simply grant that Santa gives out of his pure and natural generosity. Would that make him an ideal role model?

Maybe. But there's another possibility. Consider Dickens' famous character Scrooge. Scrooge is not exactly a generous person. He is, well, a real scrooge. But let's alter the details of the story a bit. By the end of his experience he remains the same basic character he is: grouchy, unpleasant, and decidedly ungenerous. But now the philosopher within him has reached the conclusion that being generous is a good and admirable virtue. Unlike Santa he doesn't *feel* like being generous, and he has to overcome something within him in order to be generous. But he does so because he is now guided by what is right rather than by how he feels.

So now who is more admirable: the generous person who gives easily, naturally, or the person who has to overcome even his own natural antipathy in order to act generously?

I wonder what Santa and Scrooge would say.

RELATED CHAPTERS: 5, 12

46

COOPERATING IN NOT COOPERATING

Consider the following scenario. You have arranged to make some secret purchase. You will leave some money in a small bag at a designated place, while the other person will leave the goods in a bag at another designated place. Obviously both of you face some risk: the other might leave an empty bag. And while both of you would be perfectly satisfied if the other cooperated, you'd each be even better off if the other cooperated while you defected—for then you would get the goods for no money while he would get the money for no goods. If you are trying to maximize your own gain, then the question is this: should you cooperate, or should you defect?

Well, the rational person (it seems) might reason as follows. There are only two options: either the other person, the dealer, will leave the goods or not. If the dealer leaves the goods then you would be better off not leaving the money, for then you get something for nothing. But if the dealer does not leave the goods then you'd also be better off not leaving the money, for you *avoid* getting nothing for something. So either way you're better off defecting.

But meanwhile, of course, the dealer is also thinking things through. From his perspective, there are only two options: you, the buyer, will either leave the money or not. If you leave the money then he is better off not leaving the goods, for that yields him money for nothing. But if you don't leave the money then he is also better off not leaving the goods, for then he avoids getting nothing for something. So either way *he's* better off defecting.

So two rational people have just decided they're each better off defecting, resulting in each leaving (and thus finding) empty bags at the designated places, thus getting nothing for nothing—when clearly each would have been better off had they both cooperated and thus gotten something for something, which was their original goal.

Maybe we shouldn't be so rational all the time.

RELATED CHAPTERS: 11, 14

47

COOL METAPHORS

Our language is filled to the brim with metaphors. We regularly speak (for example) of the mouth of a river, a rich dessert, or of being filled to the brim. It's hard enough, as we've seen, to make sense of the literal meanings of words such as proper names; but the problems only become bigger when we turn to the meanings of metaphors.

What meanings, exactly, do metaphors express?

One plausible idea might be this: a metaphor is an abbreviated comparison, so that the metaphorical meaning of an expression would itself be captured by a sentence literally asserting the explicit comparison. So, for example, to say "My ex is a block of ice" is to say something whose metaphorical meaning might be expressed by "My ex is *like* a block of ice." The original sentence then has two meanings: a literal one which is false ("My ex *is* a block of ice") and the metaphorical one (expressed by "My ex is *like* a block of a ice") which may well be true.

And yet this theory doesn't quite work.

For we haven't actually made sense of the metaphor, ultimately. Someone says "My ex is a block of ice," meaning, via our theory, that her ex is like a block of ice. But in what ways? Perhaps by being hard and cold—but of course her ex is not *literally* hard and cold (assuming he's alive!). We still have some metaphors there to make sense of, so again we must translate those metaphors into something like this: "My ex is *like* hard and cold things." But again, in what ways? Perhaps by being stubborn, and unemotional. But now there's no sense in which the block of ice is *literally* "stubborn" and "unemotional," at least not any more or less than any other inanimate object would be. But then, if so, we have no real explanation for why the speaker said "My ex is a block of ice" instead of saying, for example, "My ex is Barack Obama's left nostril"—for his ex is no more or less *literally* like, or unlike, either the ice or the nostril. Which means we haven't really made sense of the original metaphor.

Metaphors, it seems, are rather impenetrable.

Sort of like blocks of ice.

RELATED CHAPTERS: 6, 15, 25, 35

48

"IN ONE EAR AND OUT THE OTHER"

… my exasperated wife says when once again I've forgotten some glorious detail about her day. Her admittedly common-sense assumption here is that mental activities—such as memories, or more generally thoughts—occur "in the head." So if it doesn't stay in the head it doesn't stay in the mind.

So much for commonsense.

What is a thought? It's a mental activity that is always "about" something: politics, or atoms, or in my case about mollifying my wife. If you and I are thinking about the same thing then we have the same thought; if about different things, then different thoughts. And if thoughts are in the head, then—since brains are all that's really in the head—two people with their brains in identical states would be thinking the same thought.

But now imagine that there is another planet exactly like Earth. Same size, same shape, indeed exact molecular duplicates of everything on Earth. Even *you* have a duplicate, a Twin You! There is only one difference: what's in their lakes and falls from their clouds is not H_2O, what we call "water," but some other chemical (XYZ) that merely resembles H_2O. No one could tell the difference: XYZ looks, smells, and tastes like water, and they even call it "water"! But it wouldn't *be* water: water is H_2O, and this is XYZ.

Now you are eyeing a glass of water on Earth. Your Twin is eyeing a glass of XYZ on Twin Earth. You think: "Mmm, water." Your Twin thinks: "Mmm, water." You are having a thought about water. But although your Twin used the word "water," *his thought is not about water*. It's about the stuff in his glass, which is XYZ—and XYZ is not water.

But then you and your Twin are thinking about different things. So you are having different thoughts, as we noted above, despite the same words. But as molecular duplicates your brains are in the very same state. If thoughts were in the head, the same brain activity (which is all that's in the head) would yield the same thoughts. You two have the same brain activity but yet are thinking different thoughts.

So thoughts are not, after all, in the head—strange as that may sound.

My wife's day does not actually go in one ear and out the other, it turns out. It never gets in at all.

RELATED CHAPTERS: 4, 19, 42, 52

49

THE LUCK OF THE DRAW

"Life's not fair," many people complain—though usually only when the unfairness disadvantages them. A brief glance around does quickly reveal major disparities in all sorts of "goods": health, wealth, power, status, and so on. And there are indeed many cases where individuals may legitimately complain of unfairness.

But there is perhaps less overall unfairness than you might think.

For many disparities may be traced to a more fundamental one: the disparity of birth. Some people are born with greater intelligence than others. Some are born healthier than others. Some are born into developed countries, into financially secure families and prospering communities, while others are not. You (for example) were born with brains and money and good looks, and me, I got to bathe twice a month, together with all five of my siblings, at least when the water bill was paid. How unfair!

Or is it?

Imagine you are in some desperate situation: eleven of you on a lifeboat which can only support ten. One of you must be sacrificed so that the rest may survive. Everyone wants to survive. Everyone is as deserving as anyone else *to* survive. So how would you choose in the fairest way possible the person to be sacrificed?

You would no doubt set up some form of random lottery. Maybe a series of coin flips; a rock–paper–scissors tournament; or whoever pulls the shortest stick. If your twig came up short it would definitely be terrible, a disaster, and a catastrophe. But what it wouldn't be is unfair. Because randomness, by definition, cannot be unfair. Randomness has no bias and no prejudice; everyone has an equal opportunity, or faces an equal threat, before a genuinely random process.

So the random lottery of birth, which generates so much disparity, really may be terrible, a disaster, a catastrophe. To make for a better world we have plenty of reasons to fight against it and try to correct for it.

But not, necessarily, because it's unfair.

RELATED CHAPTERS: 5, 39

50

SOMETIMES YOU'RE JUST NOT YOURSELF

Imagine scientists have perfected teletransportation. You step into a machine which quickly scans all the molecules in your body and brain then disassembles them, since they're no longer necessary. The machine then sends the scanned information by radio to your destination. There the receiving machine reconstitutes your body/brain from its own store of molecules. And there you are, at your destination.

From your perspective you step into a machine in one place then instantly find yourself somewhere else: let's say Mars. True your body is now composed of different molecules, but even today, as we've seen, your body's molecules are constantly changing. What matters is not which molecules they are but how they are arranged, and these are arranged into *you*. In fact you telecommute daily to your job on Mars and are none the worse for it.

But now suppose one morning, after you've departed Earth, Ted the technician forgets to delete the information just scanned from you. When he next activates the machine it reads your scan and reconstitutes your body/brain from its molecule bin. From your perspective, of course, you find yourself an eyeblink after entering the machine. You see Ted's surprised face, and you say: "How about pressing the button already, buddy?"

But wait—who is saying all this? It's not you: you're already on Mars. But then again maybe he *is* you. We might even imagine he's just been constituted from the very same molecules deconstituted from you a moment before. So maybe the guy on Mars is the imposter? But wait—if the teletransported guy is not you after all then we have to say you are long gone, since you've been teletransporting daily since you got the Martian job. So he better be you. So whoever is now demanding an explanation from Ted isn't you. Unless he is?

Then the monitor flips on with an incoming video call from Mars.

Your face is on the screen. "Ted, I left my . . ."

Your eyes lock. (I mean with his. I mean with yours.)

"Who are *you*?" you both say simultaneously.

RELATED CHAPTERS: 8, 19, 22, 32, 41, 57

51

SOME ADO ABOUT NOTHING

Astronomers recently announced that they have discovered absolutely nothing. Apparently, you see, there's an enormous void a billion light-years across somewhere out there in space.

That is indeed a whole lot of nothing. And that is the problem. For how can there be a "whole lot" of something unless it *were* something?

To be sure, nothing does seem like something. We have that word for it, after all, which is a noun to boot—and don't nouns have meanings by standing for things? So if "nothing" is to mean something then nothing better *be* something.

But what kind of thing?

It's not like us, or any physical objects, which are made up of smaller things like atoms. In fact pure empty space is not composed of anything at all. It is, somehow, a thing composed of nothing.

Things also have various properties. Eyes may be blue; salt dissolves in water; water boils at 100 degrees Centigrade. Every ordinary physical thing has weight; chairs support weight. But space doesn't have a color, it doesn't dissolve or boil, it has no weight, and it supports nothing. It is, somehow, a thing that lacks those sorts of properties.

And yet it doesn't lack properties altogether. We can say how much nothing there is, as did those astronomers. We can say how long it lasts: that painful silence following your proposal of marriage lasted seven seconds (*not* an eternity). We can be moved emotionally by nothing: when the doctor reports that there's nothing in our abdomen after all, we are relieved. Nothing even has causal powers. The passerby who did nothing (instead of alerting you to the oncoming bicycle) caused the collision. If nothing can have all these properties—a size, a duration, even causal powers—it must be something.

A something which is nothing.

Admittedly, this is quite a bit of ado. But thinking about nothing is much harder than you might think. And that is not nothing. It is the absence of nothing, which is really something. Or is that everything?

RELATED CHAPTERS: 8, 40

52

THE EYEBALL OF THE BEHOLDER

A friend recently looked askance at my supper. "What?" I said. "It's delicious." "No it isn't," he replied. I didn't continue this argument since yielding meant more supper for me. But I also didn't continue because there's nothing to argue about here.

Why not? Because how things taste, like other things we've seen, is relative. Whether two objects match in color; whether a room feels warm or cool; or whether someone is beautiful, all of these vary between perceivers and we can't say any one perception is correct while the others are not. The features perceived here are subjective: not in the object but in the mind of the perceiver. Beauty, as they say, is in the eye of the beholder.

But now consider even the shape and size of an object. The coin in your hand looks round from straight on but looks oval from even a slight angle. From far away it looks small while from nearby it looks large. In all of these cases, a certain perceived quality varies between acts of perceiving while the object itself does not: it's the same coin whether it looks round or oval, or small or large. But if the perceived quality varies while the object itself does not, then the perceived quality must not be in the object. So what you perceive with respect to shape and size, too, is subjective, i.e. a sensation within your mind. But it doesn't stop here.

For what we perceive, in perceiving objects, are colors, tastes, sizes, shapes. And objects are nothing more than collections of colors, tastes, sizes, and shapes. If these latter are all just sensations in perceivers, then *so are the objects themselves*. Or to put it bluntly: It's not merely that what we perceive are sensations in minds.

It's that mental sensations are all there is.

So there are no genuinely physical objects. There are only minds and their sensations. It's not just beauty that's in the eye of the beholder, then: even the eyeball of the beholder is in the eye of the beholder.

RELATED CHAPTERS: 3, 4, 8, 9, 16, 30, 42, 48, 56

53

YOU EITHER WILL, OR WILL NOT,
BUY THIS ARGUMENT

Well, duh. You don't need a philosopher to tell you that *that* statement is true. After all there are only two options here: you either will or you will not. So you either will, or will not.

And that's all you need to know in order to know that you don't have free will.

Take any possible action of yours, such as wearing your striped blue vest tomorrow. As above you either will, or will not, wear that vest. Neither of us may know right now which will occur—perhaps we must wait to see how you feel tomorrow morning. But we do know that one of the options will occur.

So suppose it's the first one: it's true that you will wear that vest tomorrow. If it's true right now that you will wear it, then there's nothing you can do *not* to wear it. For if you could manage not to wear it then it would *not* be true that you *will* wear it, contrary to our supposition. So if the first option is correct then there's nothing you can do about it: you will wear that vest.

So suppose it's the second option: it's true that you will *not* wear the vest. But if it's true right now that you will *not* wear the vest then there's nothing you can do *to* wear it. For if you *could* manage to wear it then it would *not* be true now that you will not wear it, contrary to our supposition. So if the second option is correct there's also nothing you can do about it: you will not wear the vest.

So, no, we may not know right now which option will obtain. But we do know that one of them will, and that whichever one that is, there was nothing you could do about it. So whichever you do, you will not have done freely.

And of course the same applies to *any* possible action of yours. For either you will or will not marry that person; either you will or will not eat that dessert; and either you will or will not make a fashion faux-pas tomorrow.

It's true right now, in short, that you have no real options about anything that you do.

RELATED CHAPTERS: 10, 23, 34, 43

54

TO PLUG, OR NOT TO PLUG

Little matters more, to many people, than figuring out what really matters.

And as we've seen, a nice case can be made that nothing matters more, that we value nothing more fundamentally, than happiness. We want various things for the sake of the happiness they bring us, but happiness we want for its own sake. The genuinely moral life, correspondingly, would be one which aims to bring about the most happiness for the most people.

Except for one problem.

Imagine there were a machine which could give you any experience you desired. When you plug into it your brain is stimulated so that you enjoy whatever experiences make you happy: the feeling of basking on a warm beach, the sensations of a nice massage, or, for the heartier crowd, the experience of going for a vigorous long bicycle ride. Or perhaps you have loftier tastes, so what would make you happy would be the experiences of having a good talk with a friend, or understanding the latest advances in physics, maybe even winning the Nobel Prize. Or maybe you're, well, a little different, and would be made most happy by experiencing some suffering. *Whatever* experiences you want, you merely need to plug in and the experience machine would provide them.

Would you plug into the machine—not merely for a few minutes, but, say, for the rest of your life?

Most people, when asked, are inclined to say no. What matters to us, it seems, is not merely having certain experiences but actually *doing* various things. We want actually to do that long bicycle ride, not merely have the sensory experience of doing it. We want actually to win the Nobel Prize, not just have the experience of winning it—even if, while in the machine, we would never know otherwise. It's not merely experiences that matter: it's something more.

But then happiness must not be what we fundamentally value after all. For if it were we would all plug into the machine, which could give us whatever form of happiness we seek.

But we wouldn't.

So there's something more.

RELATED CHAPTERS: 5, 12, 20, 29, 39, 58

55

IT'S ALL ENGLISH TO ME

I recently learned that the expression "It's all Greek to me" derives from medieval philosophers bemoaning their inability to read ancient texts. That made me wonder what the *Greeks* say; which, it turns out, is "It's all Chinese me." Before investigating what the Chinese say, however, I realized I'd have a deeper problem with whatever resource I might consult: it would be all English to me. And I don't understand what understanding English amounts to.

To see why, imagine a man locked in a room. Pieces of paper with strange marks come through a slot in the door; the man consults a rule book he has (in English), and then from some boxes assembles some new marks to return out the slot. The process repeats. He doesn't understand these marks; he's just mechanically following rules matching input marks with outputs. But unbeknownst to him the marks are Chinese characters. The people on the outside are native Chinese speakers who believe they are conversing with another native speaker within.

Interestingly, now, computers are quite like the man in the room: they're purely mechanical devices which operate on electrical inputs to produce electrical outputs, all according to a program they follow mechanically. Just as the man with his rule book perfectly *simulates* an ordinary conversation, so too would a properly programmed computer. But just as the man does not actually understand any Chinese, neither does the computer understand what it is doing. Thus computers at best simulate mentality and cannot literally possess it.

This argument now raises a difficult question. It assumes that there is more to genuinely "understanding" a language than simply being able to produce appropriate outputs given various inputs. After all, the man and computer both can do the latter but fail to display the former. But *what* else is there? When *you* hear certain English sounds you know what other sounds are appropriate to produce in reply. You "genuinely understand" English. So what exactly is there to "understanding" *beyond* the ability to utter the appropriate responses?

That's what is all Urdu to me.

RELATED CHAPTERS: 4, 6, 24

56

THERE'S ... SOMETHING ...
OUT ... THERE

You know those ambiguous drawings—for example the one which looks like a young woman one way but like an old woman another way? It's tempting to wonder what that picture is of *in itself* so to speak. But of course the answer is neither, or both: it depends on how you, the perceiver, sees it.

But so does everything else.

Compare the difference between hearing a language you understand and one you don't. When you hear English you hear words or maybe even meanings; when you hear Urdu you hear only sounds. But the difference is not in your ears. Rather it's in your mind, which can interpret the former sounds and not the latter.

Similarly my cat will look at my computer and not see a computer. When he spreads out on my desk he sees neither the important papers he is pushing over the edge nor my annoyance as I push *him* over the edge. The problem isn't that he is blind. The problem is that he lacks the relevant concepts: computer, papers, etc. At most what he sees is something like a pattern of lights and colors. His limited mind cannot interpret those patterns as we who have these concepts do.

Indeed we fail to appreciate how much work our own minds do in constructing our experience of the world. The "objective" world supposedly consists of stable physical objects which have their properties "in themselves," independent of anyone's perceiving them. But your sensory experience actually gives you no such thing! What your eyes "see" strictly speaking is that vast fluctuating array of lights and colors. It's your mind, applying its concepts, which interprets those patterns—which sees them *as* a breakfast table, a banana on the floor, and the kids' dirty sneakers.

I'm not saying that there is no world outside our minds. There is; but what that world *is*, the precise objects it contains, is in some sense "up to us," up to how we, with whatever concepts we may have, interpret our sensations. Just as "what" you see when you look at an ambiguous image depends on how you look at it, so too, in other words, does what you see anywhere else. There is indeed *something* out there—but *what* it is, exactly, depends on just who's perceiving it.

RELATED CHAPTERS: 3, 4, 11, 30, 31, 33, 42, 52, 57

57

WHAT EXPERIENCE CANNOT TEACH

To be sure, much of what we know about the world we learn through sensory experience. That may tempt you to think that our minds, at birth, are like blank slates: empty of content, waiting to be filled up via experiences. But while our bodies may indeed be naked at birth, our minds in fact are not: we arrive in this world with a healthy stock of innate ideas.

The proof is the fact that we are, as adults, possessed of ideas which sensory experience itself simply could not have given us.

There are moral concepts, for example, such as "right" and "wrong." As we've seen, our senses are just not equipped to detect these sorts of things: our eyes see only light and color, not "rightness" and "wrongness."

There are mathematical concepts. Never mind the advanced ones, for even the more accessible ones, such as those of numbers, must be innate. For while we may see three oranges, or three trees, we never literally see the number three *itself*. In fact, as we've noted, numbers seem to be concepts in our mind which we apply *to* what we see, not concepts we derive *from* what we see.

We similarly have the concept of a "self," of our selves, but our senses cannot give us anything like it. We surely don't perceive it with our eyes, ears, or nose. At best we "reflect," mentally, and "look within" to discover it. But even this reflection doesn't yield it: all we're ever aware of, in fact, is an incessantly changing flux of thoughts, perceptions, memories, and so on. We're never aware of the person or self who *has* those thoughts and perceptions, who in fact is reflecting on them.

And finally there is the idea of God. You may not believe in God's existence but you still have the concept, namely that of an infinite being. But the concept of infinity surely does not derive from sensory experience, for everything we experience is finite.

Experience, then, may give us many things. But it doesn't give us what we already have within—including the infinite.

RELATED CHAPTERS: 4, 5, 7, 11, 17, 22, 31, 56

58

INTOLERANCE IS A VIRTUE

Tolerance is a virtue, or so many think. Sure such people have noble motives: different societies have different morals, they say, and we shouldn't arrogantly assume that our own morals are the only correct ones. So "let's be tolerant of differences." But this sort of universal tolerance really makes no sense. If you believe a given practice is morally wrong then you *shouldn't* tolerate it, for that would be to condone it. And if you believe that practice is morally acceptable then you're not "tolerating" it, you're agreeing with it! So if you really think a practice is wrong, you should think of it as wrong for *everyone*.

Suppose you were a teacher and you awarded different grades to two identical exams. The students would be outraged. Why? Because you awarded a difference in "value"—a different grade—where there was no underlying difference in "facts"—here, answers—to justify it. That is clearly wrong.

But those noble tolerators are doing the same thing. Westerners condemn (for example) "female genital mutilation" while various others consider it a moral obligation. A tolerator—who believes it's wrong but "tolerates" it for others—is effectively granting a difference in "value": that practice is wrong "for us" but acceptable "for them." But now what is the relevant difference in facts between the two cases to justify awarding these different values? There is none.

True, different societies have different beliefs about morality. But suppose someone believes that sex between an adult and a child is morally acceptable. No matter how nobly tolerant we might be, we wouldn't tolerate this person. Why? Because his simply *believing* that sex with children is acceptable does not make it so. Nor would it be so if this man had a dozen friends who shared his beliefs, or even a few hundred or thousand, or a whole society. Moral legitimacy is not to be found in numbers.

If you believe a practice is wrong, then, have the courage of your convictions: it is wrong for everyone.

You ought not to tolerate the tolerators.

RELATED CHAPTERS: 5, 29

59

THE BEST OF ALL POSSIBLE WORLDS

There's a philosophical joke: The optimist says, "This is the best of all possible worlds." And the pessimist agrees.

Of course by this standard most people are neither optimist nor pessimist, since it seems just obvious that this world is *not* the best possible one. Just take some little bad thing—like that joke—and imagine replacing it with a better joke. Wouldn't that be a better overall world, even if only a little? And if a better world were possible then our actual world wouldn't be the *best* possible one.

But now many think that a God who is all powerful, all knowing, and all good would create the best of all possible worlds. And so if our actual world is not the best possible world then God must not exist. That bad joke thus proves that God doesn't exist!

Or does it?

This reasoning assumes that we're in a position to judge the overall value of the world. For example, we imagine we can think of "better" worlds by eliminating unpleasant facts about our actual world. But it's not so simple. Replace that bad joke with a better one; you would then laugh for a few seconds instead of groaning for one. Okay, but then you'd leave the house later too and perhaps get into the fatal accident you wouldn't even know you missed by leaving when you did. And then the cure for cancer you were going to produce in ten years never comes into being. We don't know; we can't know.

But we don't have to. For all we know, this world is overall as good as any world could be. For all we know, any other world would actually be a worse world. So no we can't know that this *is* the best of all possible worlds—but then we can't know either that it isn't. And if we can't know that it *isn't* then the existence of this world—evils, bad jokes and all—cannot disprove the existence of God.

It may be cold comfort to recognize that God might exist *despite* all the evils. But even cold comfort is comfort.

RELATED CHAPTERS: 5, 7, 17, 26, 36, 43, 57

60

THIS IS NOT THE END

Lots of things never end. Space. Time. Numbers. The questions little kids ask.

And philosophy.

You try to convince somebody of something—even your-self—by offering reasons to believe the thing. But then your belief is only as valid as your reasons are, so you offer reasons to accept your reasons. But then those reasons need *further* reasons and you're off. As a result it often seems that there aren't any answers to philosophical questions: there are just more argu-ments, more objections, more replies. And so it may easily seem that it's not worth even getting started. Why bother? You'll never finish. You may as well try to count all the numbers.

But there is another way of thinking about it.

I went snorkeling for the first time a few years ago. It was an amazing experience. There was a whole world under that water to which I'd been oblivious my entire life. This world was populated with countless amazing creatures with all sorts of complex relationships to each other in that tangled ecosystemic way. Indeed every single thing was connected to every other thing: this one is food for that one, which excretes chemicals used by another one, which excretes waste products used by others, and so on. Stunning, fascinating, and absolutely, deeply, beautiful. It had been there all along, just waiting for me to dive in.

If you were now to tell me that that ocean goes on forever, filled with ever more amazing creatures in more amazing relationships—I wouldn't say, "Well then why bother entering?" Rather, I'd say, "Where can a guy get a wetsuit around here?"

But that is philosophy. It's filled with countless amazing ideas, concepts, beings, which exist in all sorts of complex logical relationships with each other. And unlike the actual ocean this one *is* infinitely deep: Wherever you enter you can keep going, and going, and going. What you should be thinking, then, is not: "Why enter?" It is, rather, this: thank you—very much.

But of course, that world just is *this* world, the world that you're in. This great ocean you may be looking for, you're already in it. You just have to start thinking about it. The very first drop in that bucket is a splash into the infinite.

This is the beginning.

RELATED CHAPTER: 1

SOURCES

Chapter 3

René Descartes, *Meditations on First Philosophy* (1641), "Meditation One." Reprinted in Donald Cress, ed., *Meditations on First Philosophy*, 3rd Edition (Indianapolis, IN: Hackett Publishing Company, 1993).

Chapter 7

Paul Davies, *The Mind of God* (New York: Simon and Schuster, 1992), Chapter 8: "Designer Universe."

Chapter 9

C. L. Hardin, "Color and Illusion," in William Lycan, ed., *Mind and Cognition: A Reader* (Cambridge, MA: Blackwell, 1990), 555–67.

Chapter 12

John Stuart Mill, "Utilitarianism" (1861). Reprinted in H. B. Acton, ed., *J. S. Mill's Utilitarianism, On Liberty and Considerations on Representative Government* (London: J. M. Dent & Sons, 1972).

Chapter 13

Donald Davidson, "Mental Events," in L. Foster and J. Swanson, eds., *Experience and Theory* (Humanities Press, 1970), 79–101. Reprinted in David J. Chalmers, ed., *Philosophy of Mind: Classical and Contemporary Readings* (Oxford: Oxford University Press, 2002).

   Jaegwon Kim, *Philosophy of Mind* (Boulder, CO: Westview Press, 1996), Chapter 6: "Mental Causation."

Chapter 14

Robert Nozick, "Newcomb's Problem and Two Principles of Choice," in Nicholas Rescher, ed., *Essays in Honor of Carl G. Hempel* (Dordrecht, the Netherlands: D. Reidel, 1969), 115.

Chapter 15

J. S. Mill, *A System of Logic* (New York: Harper & Brothers, 1874), Book I, Chapter II, Section 5: "Of Names." Reprinted in A. P. Martinich, *The Philosophy of Language*, 4th Edition (Oxford: Oxford University Press, 2001).

Gottlob Frege, "On Sense and Nominatum" (1892). Trans. Herbert Feigl, reprinted in A. P. Martinich, *The Philosophy of Language*, 4th Edition (Oxford: Oxford University Press, 2001).

Chapter 16

John Locke, *Essay Concerning Human Understanding* (1690), Book II, Chapter VIII.21. Reprinted in Roger Ariew and Eric Watkins, eds., *Modern Philosophy: An Anthology of Primary Sources* (Indianapolis, IN: Hackett Publishing Company, 1998).

Chapter 17

Thomas Aquinas, *Summa Theologica*, P. 1, Q. 25, 3rd article: "Whether God is Omnipotent." Trans. Fathers of the English Domincan Province (Allen, TX: Christian Classics, 1981).

Chapter 18

Bertrand Russell, "On the Notion of Cause," *Proceedings of the Aristotelian Society*, 13, 1912–13. Reprinted in John G. Slater, ed., *Bertrand Russell: Logical and Philosophical Papers 1909–1913* (London: Routledge, 1992).

Chapter 19

Frank Jackson, "Epiphenomenal Qualia," *Philosophical Quarterly*, 32, 1982, 127–36. Reprinted in David J. Chalmers, ed., *Philosophy of Mind: Classical and Contemporary Readings* ⟨...⟩ ᵣd University Press, 2002).

⟨...⟩w, Yujin Nagasawa, and Daniel Stoljar, eds., ⟨...⟩ *About Mary: Essays on Phenomenal Consciousness* ⟨...⟩*n's Knowledge Argument* (Cambridge, MA: ⟨...⟩4).

⟨...⟩ıson, "The Trolley Problem," *The Yale Law* ⟨...⟩*y*, 1985, 1395–415.

⟨...⟩furt, "Alternate Possibilities and Moral Responsᵢ⟨...⟩," *The Journal of Philosophy*, 66(23), 4 December 1969, 829–39.

Chapter 24

A. M. Turing, "Computing Machinery and Intelligence," *Mind*, LIX, 236, 1950. Reprinted in Douglas R. Hofstadter and Daniel C. Dennett, eds., *The Mind's I: Fantasies and Reflections on Self and Soul* (Toronto, CA: Bantam Books 1981).

Douglas R. Hofstadter, "A Coffeehouse Conversation on the Turing Test to Determine if a Machine Can Think," *Scientific American*, May 1981, 15–36. Reprinted in Douglas R. Hofstadter and Daniel C. Dennett, eds., *The Mind's I: Fantasies and Reflections on Self and Soul* (Toronto, CA: Bantam Books 1981).

Chapter 26

Plato, "Euthyphro" (fourth century B.C.E.). Reprinted in John M. Cooper, ed., *Plato: Complete Works* (Indianapolis, IN: Hackett Publishing Company, 1997).

Chapter 27

Carl G. Hempel, "Studies in the Logic of Confirmation," *Mind*, 54, 1945, 1–26, 97–121. Reprinted in Carl G. Hempel, *Aspects of Scientific Explanation and Other Essays in the Philosophy of Science* (New York: The Free Press, 1965).

Chapter 30

René Descartes, *Meditations on First Philosophy* (1641), "Meditation One." Reprinted in Donald Cress, ed., *Meditations on First Philosophy*, 3rd Edition (Indianapolis, IN: Hackett Publishing Company, 1993).

Chapter 32

D. M. Armstrong, *Universals: An Opinionated Introduction* (Boulder, CO: Westview Press, 1989).

Chapter 33

George Berkeley, *Three Dialogues between Hylas and Philonous* (1713), "The First Dialogue." Reprinted in Roger Ariew and Eric Watkins, eds., *Modern Philosophy: An Anthology of Primary Sources* (Indianapolis, IN: Hackett Publishing Company, 1998).

Chapter 34

Richard Taylor, *Metaphysics*, 4th Edition (New Jersey: Prentice Hall, 1963/1992), Chapter 6: "Fate."

Chapter 35

John Searle, "Proper Names," *Mind*, 67, 1958, 166–73. Reprinted in A. P. Martinich, *The Philosophy of Language*, 3rd Edition (Oxford, UK: Oxford University Press, 1996).

Chapter 36

René Descartes, *Meditations on First Philosophy* (1641), "Meditation Three." Reprinted in Donald Cress, ed., *Meditations on First Philosophy*, 3rd Edition (Indianapolis, IN: Hackett Publishing Company, 1993).

Chapter 37

David Hume, *An Inquiry Concerning Human Understanding* (1748), Section IV. Reprinted in Roger Ariew and Eric

Watkins, eds., *Modern Philosophy: An Anthology of Primary Sources* (Indianapolis, IN: Hackett Publishing Company, 1998).

Chapter 38

David Hume, *An Inquiry Concerning Human Understanding* (1748), Section IV. Reprinted in Roger Ariew and Eric Watkins, eds., *Modern Philosophy: An Anthology of Primary Sources* (Indianapolis, IN: Hackett Publishing Company, 1998).

Chapter 40

Augustine, *Confessions* (397 C.E.), Book 11. Reprinted in Jonathan Westphal and Carl Levenson, eds., Hackett Readings in Philosophy: *Time* (Indianapolis, IN: 1993).

Chapter 41

G. W. Leibniz (1646–1716) on the "Indiscernibility of Identicals." See H. G. Alexander, ed., *The Leibniz–Clarke Correspondence* (Manchester: Manchester University Press, 1956), L.IV.3–6.

Chapter 46

Douglas Hofstadter, "The Prisoner's Dilemma and the Evolution of Cooperation," in *Metamagical Themas: Questing for the Essence of Mind and Pattern* (New York: Basic Books, 1985).

Chapter 47

John Searle, "Metaphor," in A. Ortony, ed., *Metaphor and Thought* (Cambridge: Cambridge University Press, 1979). Reprinted in J. R. Searle, *Expression and Meaning* (Cambridge: Cambridge University Press, 1979).

William Lycan, *Philosophy of Language: A Contemporary Introduction* (London: Routledge, 1999), Chapter 14: "Metaphor."

Chapter 48

Hilary Putnam, "The Meaning of 'Meaning,'" in Keith Gunderson, ed., *Language, Mind, and Knowledge*, Minnesota Studies in the Philosophy of Science (Minneapolis, MN: University of Minnesota Press), vol. VII, 131–93.

Andrew Pessin and Sanford Goldberg, eds.; *The Twin Earth Chronicles: Twenty Years of Reflection on Hilary Putnam's "The Meaning of 'Meaning'"* (Armonk, NY: M. E. Sharpe, 1996).

Chapter 50

Derek Partfit, *Reasons and Persons* (Oxford: Oxford University Press, 1984), Chapter 10: "What We Believe Ourselves to Be."

Chapter 52

George Berkeley, *Three Dialogues between Hylas and Philonous* (1713), "The First Dialogue." Reprinted in Roger Ariew and

Eric Watkins, eds., *Modern Philosophy: An Anthology of Primary Sources* (Indianapolis, IN: Hackett Publishing Company, 1998).

Chapter 53

Aristotle (384–322 B.C.E.), *De Interpretatione*, Chapter 9. In J. L. Ackrill, ed., *A New Aristotle Reader* (Princeton, NJ: Princeton University Press, 1987).

Chapter 54

Robert Nozick, "The Experience Machine," in *Anarchy, State, & Utopia* (New York: Basic Books, 1974), 42–5.

Chapter 55

John Searle, "Minds, Brains, and Programs," *Behavioral and Brain Sciences*, 3, 1980, 417–58. Reprinted in John Perry and Michael Bratman, eds., *Introduction to Philosophy: Classical and Contemporary Readings*, 3rd Edition (Oxford: Oxford University Press, 1999).

Chapter 59

G. W. Leibniz, *Theodicy: Essays on the Goodness of God and the Freedom of Man and the Origin of Evil* (1710), "Summary of the Controversy Reduced to Formal Arguments." Reprinted in Austin Farrer, ed., E. M. Huggard trans., *G. W. Leibniz: Theodicy* (La Salle, IL: Open Court, 1985).

INDEX

The God Question

What famous thinkers from Plato to Dawkins have said about the divine

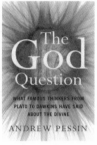

9781851686599
£9.99/ $14.95

For centuries, our greatest philosophers, from Aristotle to Nietzsche, have sought to clarify the idea of a Supreme Being and examine the unique conundrums that He raises. Presenting pithy arguments from the faithful, atheistic, and downright heretical, Pessin's light-hearted prose will give you a captivating insight into a wide array of God-related puzzles, whether or not you are religiously inclined.

"A really excellent book - next to faultless in its presentation."
Tim Mawson – Lecturer in Philosophy, University of Oxford

"Brilliantly succinct. If you want to know what the greatest minds of the past 2500 years said on the most contentious issue in all of culture, you simply must start with this book."
Michael Shermer – Founding Publisher of Skeptic Magazine and author of *Why People Believe Weird Things*

ANDREW PESSIN is Chair of Philosophy at Conneticut College. He is the author of *Gray Matters: An Introduction to the Philosophy of Mind* and has appeared on the David Letterman show several times as "The Genius".

Browse further titles at
www.oneworld-publications.com

The Electric Toilet Virgin Death Lottery

And Other Outrageous Logic Problems

9781851686926
£7.99/ $12.95

From FeelGoodButtGone, the antidepressant-diet-pill popular among "big-boned housewives", to taxidermists hunting penguin-bison hybrids, Cassidy and Byrne serve up a ferociously funny compendium of crazed logic puzzles and crackpot inventions. Explaining the best tactics to cracking their fiendish conundrums, as well as including step-by-step clues and answers to all the logical puzzles inside, the book promises to hone your brain into a finely-tuned instrument of unstoppable logic – as long as it doesn't burn you out in the process. Be warned!

Solve the final puzzle for a chance to win £1000 and find yourself featured in the sequel!

THOMAS CASSIDY is former Vice-Principal of Paddington Academy and founder of the CILCUS English Centre in Hong Kong.

THOMAS BYRNE is a keen puzzler and student.

Can a Robot Be Human?
33 Perplexing Philosophical Puzzles

9781851686476
£7.99/ $12.95

In this fun and entertaining book of puzzles and paradoxes, Peter Cave introduces some of life's most important questions with tales and tall stories, reasons and arguments, common sense and bizarre conclusions. From speedy tortoises to getting into heaven, paradoxes and puzzles give rise to some of the most exciting problems in philosophy—from logic to ethics and from art to politics.

"This is a chirpy introduction to philosophy through thought-experiments and paradoxes." *The Guardian*

"Lightly written, but definitely no dumbing down. A simulating read, the subject ranges wide and far." *Publishing News*

"With its wonderful varied selection of topics, plus Cave's admirable lightness of touch, this is one of the most entertaining and thought provoking books I've come across in years. So stop messing around with trivia like Sudoku and give your brain a real treat by buying this book." *Focus Magazine*

PETER CAVE regularly lectures in philosophy for The Open University and City University, London. He frequently contributes to philosophy journals and magazines, from the serious to the fun, lectures around the world, and has scripted and presented philosophy programmes for the BBC.

Browse further titles at
www.oneworld-publications.com

What's Wrong With Eating People?
33 More Perplexing Philosophical Puzzles

9781851686209
£7.99/ $12.95

In this stunning sequel to *Can a Robot be Human?*, Peter Cave once again engages the reader in a romp through the best bits of philosophical thought. With the aid of tall stories, jokes, common sense and bizarre insights, Cave tackles some of life's most important questions and introduces the puzzles that will keep you pondering throughout the night.

"Cave is not just a very gifted philosopher, he's also clear, captivating and funny too." Stephen Law – Author of *The Philosophy Gym* and editor of *Think*

"Energetic, highly entertaining, and delightfully thought-provoking." A.W. Moore – Professor of Philosophy, University of Oxford, and author of *The Infinite*

"Delightfully written and fun to read. The writing is witty and eloquent and the puzzles are explored throughout with both common sense and wisdom." Anthony Ellis – Professor of Philosophy in Virginia Commonwealth University

PETER CAVE regularly lectures in philosophy for The Open University and City University, London. He frequently contributes to philosophy journals and magazines, from the serious to the fun, lectures around the world, and has scripted and presented philosophy programmes for the BBC.

31901046586055

Browse further titles at
www.oneworld-publications.com